HOW CHRISTIAN PARENTS FACE FAMILY PROBLEMS

HOW
CHRISTIAN PARENTS
FACE
FAMILY PROBLEMS

by

JOHN   CHARLES   WYNN

Philadelphia

THE WESTMINSTER PRESS

To Rachel

Helpmeet Through
the Years of Parenthood
with Our Delightful Problems

CONTENTS

FOREWORD: SETTING A FEW THINGS STRAIGHT

THIS BOOK has been written from the scrimmage line, and not in the grandstand. As parents, we are down on the playing field where the problems somehow have to be tackled. Our concerns, let it be shamelessly stated, involve some of the very topics that appear in the chapters that follow: finances, discipline, and worship, to name a few. Whatever hereinafter follows in the way of description is real. A parent of three young children simply does not write of family relations in an ivory tower; he is spared any such seclusion.

But these chapters are also presented with a firm conviction — that although the Christian family *is* plagued by the selfsame concerns that attack nearly every other home, its reaction can be substantially different. Christianity brings into family life special insights and enables us to grasp onto divine resources. There is a way of meeting family opportunities and crises with faith.

No mere book, be it said forthrightly, makes a home Christian. Even reading the Bible cannot alone accomplish so high a goal. The plain fact is that there are no techniques or formulas known that will bring about Christian family living. It is just not to be achieved by good works alone. *The essential increment is the grace of God.* For the family like the individual is justified by faith.

9

This book is not meant to cover all the problems that a Christian parent might encounter. Nor is everything said that could be said about even these ten topics chosen. In the first part I have dealt with some of the day-by-day concerns of Christian family living, and in part two with several special problems. The reason behind the selection of topics in Part II (dealing with sex instruction, the broken home, interfaith dating patterns among our young people, and handicaps in children) is that counseling and correspondence with perplexed parents have shown these to be matters of frequent and genuine concern. Most parents need only a start to get moving into their solutions to family problems, using their own common sense and native intelligence. These will carry them far beyond the counsel of any book. Skills can be developed in problem solving; adeptness can be developed in family relations. Providentially most parents manage to grow in their abilities; they learn much from their children.

Today there is a spate of literature about the family. A great amount of it is already available in our current publications representing the secular point of view. There is no end of need, however, for literature that relates family living to the framework of Christianity. If this work makes some little contribution toward that need, I ask no more.

To the Board of Christian Education of the Presbyterian Church in the United States of America, I am profoundly grateful not only for permission to reprint sizable sections from my articles, herein altered and augmented, that first appeared in the Faith and Life curriculum, but also for the opportunity to be working in the fascinating area of family life in the first place. (Much of the material in this book has been published in a somewhat different form in the magazines *Crossroads* and *Opening Doors* and is reproduced here with permission.) Another acknowledgment of thanks is owed to the editor of *Presbyterian Life,* Robert J. Cadigan, whose permission was granted to reprint here some of the author's material that first appeared in that journal; it too has been substantially rewritten.

To those who have been of aid in the preparation of this book I extend my hearty gratitude: George L. Hunt offered invaluable counsel; Mrs. Douglas Houston carefully typed the manuscript and cared for a host of details; my wife, Rachel, as always proved an inspiration at every step.

Lastly and lovingly I set down here my inexpressible thanks to three little people who have been in and out of my study while I have attempted to write these pages. Without them I should hardly be so aware of the problems that other parents also have. They are Mark, Maryan, Martha. God bless them!

J. C. WYNN.

CHRISTIAN FAMILY RELATIONS DAY BY DAY

1: PERFECT PARENTS
JUST DON'T EXIST

Having a Christian home means far more than a houseful of nice people who treat each other fairly kindly and who go to church fairly regularly. It means a home where Christ is known and loved and served; where children come to know him through their parents; where Christian training of the children is placed ahead of the social ambition of the mother and the business ambition of the father; where the father is determined to carry on his business in conformity with the mind of Christ; where both Father and Mother are determined to make their social life conform to high Christian ideals; and where eyes see far horizons of a world to be won for Christ.
— *Paul Calvin Payne, in* Beyond Courage, *1944.*

WHOEVER glibly recites these days that worn-out adage about every man being king in his own castle just isn't thinking about modern fathers! And as for Mother occupying a pedestal, it is seemingly only to sport a chic dunce cap, if you should happen to ask her offspring. Browbeaten by the cartoonists, and an easy butt for the radio comedians' jokes, the modern parent is less often pictured as tyrant than as tyrannized. With Ogden Nash he would aver in an ironic couplet:

> "Children aren't happy with nothing to ignore
> So that's what parents were created for."

15

But we wouldn't change it for anything! It's just that many of us, being not quite certain how to go about this job of parental responsibility, wish for a greater skill and insight.

The disconcerting thing we soon learn about our child is that he is imitating his parents' ways and lines of thought. Try as we may, with all that we do for our children, they still grow up to be pretty much like their folks. The boys mimic their fathers, both consciously and unconsciously, and daughters develop their conception of men from what Daddy is like. The girls imitate Mother; and this same mother is always her son's first love, the prototype by whom he will judge future girl friends. Someday the choice of a life partner is going to be influenced (probably without their realizing it) by their good and bad recollections of life with their parents. We think sometimes we don't influence the younger generation very much; actually, children land at just about the spot we have led them!

This frightening thought carries some inferences to ponder. Those chance bits of conversation overheard by our children — what impressions do they leave? Our prejudices and convictions — would we wish them all to be caught and copied in these little lives? This matter of Christian training — what difference does it make which Bible stories we tell them at bedtime if they see us living daily as if we had never opened the dust-covered Book?

On the other hand, this conviction carries with it certain consolation. For if our main job of teaching is in what we are instead of in what we say, we have fewer details about which to worry. Rather we have a different responsibility; and that is to make certain that we live exemplary lives. If we teach through acting natural, our nature must be worthy of imitation.

One of the parent's most essential jobs, you see, is just *being* a parent. If Father *never* speaks to his son as man to man, if he lets *all* the precious experiences of prayer with his children be delegated to his wife, if he neglects *entirely* to play croquet with the kids or to construct model airplanes with them, he is still a powerful teacher. If Mother is so burdened with duties that she cannot stop for paper dolls, or finger painting, or to listen to the newest acquisition of a record collection, still she can be of immense influence just in her attitude. For good or for ill, what we are often drowns out anything we try to say.

Understanding Through Companionship

But not all solutions are complex. Just reserving time to be with their children has accomplished much for unnumbered Dads and Mothers. Of course, it involves some sacrifice, giving up a Saturday afternoon golf game, skipping a lodge dinner, maybe foregoing some evening business and so making a bit less money. Or it may mean on the distaff side less bridge, fewer club meetings, and more sharing with the children. But it's well worth it.

Story time becomes a great experience for parents and the youngsters alike. Whether it be a story manufactured from the whole cloth, an adventure tale read from a book, or a reading from the child's church school curriculum, it means a treat for the small fry. It also means that an easily accessible doorway is opened to character education. Numerous books and stories are available in bookshops, public libraries, and even in food stores. Guidance in their choice can be had for the asking. The librarian, the public-school teacher, and editors of children's magazines are expert.

Spending time together makes possible other experiences: games and contests that help teach sportsmanship and good-natured losing; working cheerfully side by side on household chores; or simply sitting in the back yard for an earnest talk. It isn't the number of hours a father spends weekly with his kiddies that counts so much as it is what goes on in the time they are together. So too the quality of Mother's time with her little ones is as important as the quantity.

Taking time with our sons and daughters implies unplanned moments as well as the organized periods. It can involve laying aside the newspaper to answer a question, or seizing some golden instant for a vitally serious explanation because a question has opened the way. It can be as brief as a smile, or time taken out to enjoy a joke together. What is essential is that the experience indicates a parent's love.

Completely bad parents are actually newsworthy items. Many pull off foolish blunders. Universally, they are known for losing their tempers when, fatigued by something at the office or in the kitchen, they fly off the handle at equally tired and irritable children. With mistaken judgment, they sometimes play favorites among their sons or daughters. They may be grossly unwise in discipline. Yet by and large, most fathers and mothers do try hard. They are aware that their children have rights, that they are important as personalities themselves. Where this respect for the personhood of the child is a part of a loving relationship in the family the child has a good start in life.

In the thirteenth century Frederick II reportedly conducted a famous and foolish experiment. Determined to learn what would be the natural language spoken by a child if he were not first taught by hearing words, he contrived to have a group of newborn and unwanted babies cared for by nurses who were under strict orders to be kind to the babies in a technical way, giving them all the normal care of feeding and clean clothing, warmth and protection, but never to speak to them or to speak in their presence; nor were they to show them any affection.

Unfortunately, the monarch never discovered what language the untutored children would speak (he evidently had a suspicion that they might somehow be born with a classical language instead of their Germanic tongue), for all the infants died. It is reported that " they could not live without the appreciation, the facial expression and friendly gestures and loving care of their nurses."

Families with their love and care are a necessary part of living. The Sixty-eighth Psalm assures us that in the scheme of things " God setteth the solitary in families." The family group holds within its very considerable power the opportunity to help its members face life courageously and with Christian convictions.

Several years ago Dr. Lauretta Bender had an article in *Child Study* entitled " There's No Substitute for Family Life." Pointing out that in her work at Bellevue Hospital in New York she sees many homeless babies cared for expertly and later placed in model homes, she nonetheless expressed anxiety that such children can sometimes become crippled personalities, and stuporous, or that they may languish and die. Even in those cases where an institutional baby has made a fair adjustment to life, it is acknowledged that he could have done much better had he had the blessings of family life. These children may not be so able to help themselves as children do in families. They may develop speech defects, mental slowness, a social attitude of suspicion, impulsive selfishness, or withdrawal. They may even be retarded in the motor activities of their arms and legs. They have no idea of how family relationships operate or even what a home is like. Such children suffering from affection hunger may always show some scars resulting from this early training which, because it was in an institution, lacked the affection of the family home.

World War II brought many surprises. One of the great surprises was a side light of the evacuation program in English cities during the blitz. When the facts were in and the results assembled, it became apparent that the pre-school children who had remained with their mothers in London and other great cities and had gone through the terror of the bombings were somehow in better mental health than those who had been evacuated to the safer zones of rural Britain! Those children under five who had been forced to undergo terrible ordeals seemed to have a miraculous reserve as long as they were not compelled to endure separation. The child above five years of age made a better adjustment to his wartime environment if, in his evacuation point, he could see something of his own experience, and could find habits that he could associate with home and Mother.

Psychiatrists and therapists are doing a remarkable work today in helping minds to find themselves. But the finest work in mental health is accomplished within the family. Families not only make personality problems; but they also solve them.

Candor compels us to admit that all parents produce their share of mistakes. The perfect parent simply doesn't exist. Father punishes too severely; Mother pampers and spoils the baby; or both of them neglect to care for such important details as family recreation or valuable learning experiences. What then? Shall we assume with the fallacious notion of the determinists that our errors in the first three years of baby's life or the preschool period (there seem to be different ways of stating it) will scar his personality for all of life? Or shall we take courage and confess that we the parents are finite, prone to mistakes and ofttimes slothful in good?

If we can own up to our fallible nature with honesty, we can make better guides to the young. We simply are more lovable as frank human beings who have foibles than as frustrated perfectionists, ever nagging and scowling. Moreover, we establish a better companionship with our children if we acknowledge that we also have our faults.

Reuel Howe, author of *Man's Need and God's Action*, has a most suggestive idea in his statement concerning parental love. In essence he says this: we parents are frequently admonished: " Love your children and all will be well." But this we cannot do, and particularly at that moment when our children most need our love, precisely because they are then least lovable. When rebellious and antagonistic, they are more likely to attract our retaliation than our love. Yet, poor parents that we are, we should be guiding them by loving-kindness instead of showing our temper.

Because we are unable to meet the heavy demands on our love, our children can never receive an adequate love and security from us. That must come from elsewhere — from a forever-loving Creator. If we could supply such infinite love, Dr. Howe goes on to say, our children would never need Christ as Saviour! We parents would fill that role. The truth, however, is that both our children *and* we ourselves need redemption, and we can acknowledge it together.

In the long run, many mistakes that parents make do

become corrected through a loving relationship. The growing child may not be able to recall the specific foibles of his parents; but he will know whether there is love in his family. While it should be pointed out for the comfort of parents that love does have a way of compensating for errors, the Christian parent must never forget that the source of all loving relationship is God in Christ.

Christian homes, let it be said again, are not the result of doing a long list of specific chores. There is no formula known by which families can mix worship, conversation, study, and tradition and thereby produce a Christian family. Families, no less than the individuals within them, are justified by their faith rather than by works. It is the grace of God, and nothing less, that overpowers our blundering ways and gives to us the means to bring our families into a Christian relationship.

Yet the reminder of the book of James illuminates the other side of the truth. Obviously, "faith without works is dead." And the bald fact is that whatever excuse they may choose for their action (and there are many ingenious excuses given), a shocking number of parents do shirk their God-given duty.

Too often in the modern home, important functions of the parents have been wished off on outside agencies. It is as if reproduction and physical care were their entire obligation. Today's secular family has been happy enough to place all the burden of education upon the public schools. They have been eager to see Scouts, the "Y's," and other clubs take over the recreation of their children. They have allowed the church and its Sunday schools to shoulder the major (and too often the only) role in the religious education of their children. Many families actually suppose that by these measures they have taken care of their responsibilities. In some cases where parents do not at all wish to shove such responsibilities onto community agencies, the organization of society nonetheless compels it.

In our era a new profession has sprung out of this tendency. This is the work of the so-called sitter. The services of a sitter were relatively unknown in America a short time ago. Now upon the chance of finding a sitter hang many major decisions about social life, family life, and community participation. A sitter has grown important to us because most families no longer live with their grandparents as the old rural pattern had it, or even in the same community as commonly happened a generation ago. There were always adults around the family circle who could care for the young when their parents were away on business or pleasure. Now families have been scattered all over the country, and because of today's business practice and modern transportation they move often. The services of someone to care for children as proxy parents has become essential.

These modern trends have encouraged some unwise parents to abdicate many of their most precious privileges. They have so come to rely upon the community, the school, and the church to care for the needs of their children that many have reduced their own participation very nearly to a level of the economic and physical. It is reminiscent of the system Plato advised in his book *The Republic*. It was that philosopher's theory that elite children should be removed from their mothers soon after birth and then be placed in a state nursery. They would attend the state school, studying ethics, mathematics, politics, and other courses while living in a communal settlement. They would have no contact with their parents or even know who they were. Subsequently, after vigorous, careful training, these children were to grow up to become the well-prepared philosopher-kings of the state!

The modern nation of Israel has had communal boarding schools where children are insulated from their working parents much of the time. In America our boarding schools are generally private and expensive. It is well-known that some children are placed in them by parents who desire to get them off their hands. No more encouraging are the additional evidences to be found in summer camps, in motion-picture houses, and on street corners that numerous mothers and fathers would welcome an arrangement that would free them of their heavy obligations.

Families today are pervaded by what the Church calls secularism. Their deep concern for economic standing and monetary returns, their predilection for commercial entertainment, their practical atheism (they live as if there is no God) are indications of the widespread secularism of our time. Fully twenty-seven million children under the age of eighteen receive practically no religious education whatsoever in the U.S.A. today. It has been suggested that our values in this day are as if someone had sneaked into a department store during the night and changed the price tags from one item to another, so that expensive items have cheap price tags and valueless articles are priced exorbitantly high. Secularism is like that. It places a premium on the unimportant and the ephemeral, passing lightly over the things that abide. American homes today reflect this vast moral confusion.

We may in humorous vein agree that Ogden Nash is correct in his assertion that parents were created so that children could ignore them. Our experiences as parents often bear this out. But our real calling as parents is to fulfill the will of God in relationship to the child he has placed in our hands. When one stops to think about it, it is an amazing thing that God should have chosen fumbling amateurs to carry out the most important task in the world: that of rearing the young " in the nurture and admonition of the Lord." Our wisdom would have dictated some other arrangement; but he " moves in a mysterious way his wonders to perform." Having chosen parents to do the job, he does not leave them alone with it. To God they can look for help and strength. To him Christian parents lift their prayers.

2: LEARNING TO COPE
WITH FAMILY CONFLICTS

Cost what it may, break the child down to obedience to the first command. And when this is once done, if you are careful never to let disobedience escape punishment of some kind or other, and punishment shall be triumphant, you will find it not difficult to maintain your absolute authority.

— The Mothers' Magazine, *1834*.

NINETEENTH century child management (the emphasis is on the word " management ") was a process of parent domination, and no fooling. In the Victorian Era, which colored all the latter years of that century, the family was regularly pictured in tintypes as a somber group surrounding the commanding figure of Father and an omniscient Mother who always knew best. The family of the tintype was invariably described as happy, its relationships as without a blemish. Grandfather never thought of challenging this system in his day; if he questioned it at all, he kept such shocking thoughts to himself.

Everyone secretly knew that married people quarreled, that children rebelled against their parents, that brothers and sisters squabbled. Yet the myth of the family in the tintype persisted because the rules prohibited mentioning any discord. Resentments were repressed because they were labled as wicked feelings. Today we grin at the prudery

26

of that day; but the reluctance to admit that there was such a thing as sex was no more characteristic of Victorianism than this notion that intrafamily conflict dare not be acknowledged. The result, we can gauge from our vantage of hindsight, was predictable: whenever a family was actually confronted with some serious dispute it stood in danger of breaking. How could it cope with the condition of conflict when it had never openly recognized that the conflict existed?

The myth of the ever-placid family has been replaced by a more honest description of home life just as definitely as the tintype has been outdated by the modern motion picture that shows all three dimensions. The family is also revealed in greater depth now than then.

For one thing we candidly admit that a certain amount of hostility is to be expected in normal family relations. Benefited by a better understanding of psychology we can even take some comfort in the turmoil of domestic bickering. It gives every one of us a chance to let off steam in the company of people who are predisposed to forgive us because they love us. This safety valve can be a valuable release for pent-up resentments that could not be expressed elsewhere.

We've learned a thing or two about this hostility. We now see that each person is capable of ambivalence, which is a psychological term for that contrary feeling that permits two opposite emotions to be harbored at once in the same person. As the refrain of a popular song has phrased it: "Sometimes I love you, sometimes I hate you." The child who screams at his mother, "I hate you, I hate you!" may mean it, and yet love and depend upon her at precisely that some moment. Candor compels the admission that parents can lovingly detest their own children too.

The realization of this possibility will smooth over many a household crisis. When Mother can take turbulent Janie into her lap and say: " I know how you feel. I can hardly stand you at times, too," something happens between them that is far more wholesome than any circumstance that would leave Mother dominating and triumphantly punishing Janie. It augurs well for both of them also in the years ahead.

The animosities of children are natural enough. We adults arouse them! For the child, his world is one big " No." Born to dependence, he begins as a helpless infant with " no language but a cry." His first frustrations come with experiencing delays in his cries for food, for warmth, or for cleanliness. But with time he will know many more. It's an adult world, and children reluctantly learn it. Even while they need the ministrations of their parents, they chafe against this dependence. Human babies are really born prematurely; it is years before they can fend for themselves. In the bird family, by contrast, is the oyster catcher whose young are scampering over the sand and grubbing for marine food a few hours after hatching.

In time, the complicated structure of family and social relations imposes yet other limits upon the child. There are rules of safety, impositions of sanitation, unreasonable demands about courtesy and co-operation. These parental assaults continue through the phases of toilet training, table manners, schoolwork, dating rules, curfews, and permission to drive the family car. It's a hard world.

Parents have their troubles too. Long misunderstood by their children, they must still persist through the years, protecting, directing, objecting. It's hardly a popular role. Ask any parent — Father and Mother find it necessary to make a great many concessions. They soon learn that children are individuals in their own rights, and not just extensions of parental personalities. They come to see that the aggression each child expresses is a wholesome thing; but they also feel its sting. Gradually the intelligent parent comes to realize that he cannot indefinitely impose his own way. Nagging is a futile device; punishment is often a Pyrrhic victory.

The children meanwhile are measuring their abilities to get along in the world. To do this they must try their offensive plays — and they have many. Most of these acts are covered by the term " aggression," a derivative from the Latin and meaning literally " pressing forward." Aggression is essential to personality growth. It is a development of won't-power. Without it a boy's or girl's future is anything but promising.

It is a curious thing that this quality of obstinacy against which parents spend so much effort and concern is a prime necessity in character growth; for unless character is fortified with a healthy stubbornness, it is flimsy stuff easily upset by a modicum of opposition.

The home, dear institution that it is, happens to be just the place for aggression to flex its muscles. Ascribe to this fact the squabbles, the tantrums, the furies of domestic life. These are also characteristic of Christian homes and need not be any disgrace. So much is demanded of members of the family. Somehow they must patiently endure violations of privacy, conflicts of wills, demands to share, frustration of desires, clashes of counterpurposes. Yet into this area of conflict, order must be introduced and love is supposed to reign. The wonder of it is that there is as much peace as there is in our homes under such circumstances.

Aggression takes peculiar twists. Psychologists agree that

the male of the species has more of it than the female: just watch the boys fight. It can be turned inward instead of outward; when it is, we label it self-control. However annoying the aggressiveness may become, it is a normal drive. The condition really to worry about is its absence. Rejoice not that a child is a " good " child, sweetly obedient and easily managed. Rather be concerned; the child who displays no aggressiveness may become a difficult problem. The smothering of this troublesome quality is neither psychologically desirable nor religiously blessed. The trick, of course, is to learn to control aggressive drives, and to devise ways of living with conflict. For this, there is no proving ground superior to the family.

One of the most dramatic parables in the whole repertoire of Jesus concerns a bitter rivalry between two brothers and their patient father's love. Jealousy and friction between siblings (a sexless term indicating either brother or sister) are universal in the world of time and space. That theme is treated in classical mythology, explored in psychology, developed in literature, and practiced in numberless families. The Japanese sum it up in a cryptic proverb: " My brother, a stranger."

Every child sometimes feels the smarting sensation of jealousy. If he's the eldest, the arrival of a new baby is the occasion for behavior problems and feelings of baffling insecurity. If he's the youngest, he sees the older children with privileges thus far denied to him and whimpers that they get all the breaks. If he's somewhere between, he's likely to feel that he's caught in the middle between older siblings who are allowed more freedom and the younger " who gets away with everything."

The child from a larger family has countless advantages. He gets the rough edges rubbed off early. He enjoys the protection and loyalty of the family group. He learns faster because he has more tutors. But you'd have to prove it to him. His impression is tinged with hand-me-down clothes, embarrassing comparisons with siblings who excel in scholarship or athletics, or the nuisance of having to look out for an annoying kid sister.

This could be serious. It is possible for brother and sister conflicts to last a lifetime. The opportunity for nipping them in the bud is while the children are young. Parents can make careful preparations for the new baby, orienting an older child gradually to the idea. Each child can be helped to find his own place, quite independent of the attainments of another child in other fields. Susie may be graceful in ballet dancing; but Sandra can find her forte in dramatics. Wise parents will often show each child some individual attention, assuring him of love and security. They will not charge older children with the task of constantly caring for younger members of the family. They will accept jealousy as a normal thing, not forcing the jealous child to feel guilty also, but helping him to overcome his jealousy with love and understanding.

There are worse things than a hot display of jealousy. A youngster could suppress these feelings, driving his bitterness down deep inside him in order to seek parental favor. But they may also crop out again many years later, paying back the original emotion with compound interest.

Jealousy is an insidious emotion, breaking up families and damaging the love relationship. It is a mistake, however, to assume that the problem is limited to children. Adults are also deeply involved. The young father who resents all the time and attention his wife gives the baby is exhibiting jealousy. The hostility between husband and wife, so common among family problems, is related to jealousy. Family friction knows no age limits, follows no logic.

One well-known study on child care found on the bookshelves of countless homes has come to be dubbed " the consolation book." To it desperate parents have turned again and again only to learn that their children's outrageous behavior just happens to be normal at that age. We find comfort in learning that numerous other families have been over this territory before and that they lived through it. A familiarity with the characteristics of a particular age aids us in knowing what to expect, and prepares us to be patient with the foibles of, say, a five-year-old. Such knowledge may guard us against expecting too much.

Unconditional obedience is a response that probably comes only from a fear-ridden coward in the face of an absolute dictator. Instances are fortunately rare in which this situation is found between children and parents. Problems of obedience are frequent and often upsetting. Ways are known, however, to reduce these problems to a lesser frequency.

For one thing, parents can refrain from making unnecessary demands on their children. They can ration their commands to include only those matters which are essential; then obedience in these can be expected. To force continual demands upon the youngsters is to risk an increase in disobedience even in the face of the most serious and essential matters. When it is advisable to issue commands, there are approved ways of doing it. Control your tone of voice. Keep it friendly; if you don't, it is possible to earn compliance and resentment at the same time. Give reasons for your commands. A child who understands is likely to be more co-operative. Make allowances for individual differences. The young person may have limitations or ideas of his own for which it is reasonable to expect tolerance. Anyway, the perfectionist parent makes life miserable for those around him.

The patient parent learns to hold his fire. He may even learn by the painful method of trial and error. Ernest G. Osborne, in *The Family Scrapbook,* cites the case of the mother who jumped to conclusions.

" Johnny had been a little disorderly now and then when he visited his friends' houses. So when he was invited to a party, his mother said, ' Johnny, if you get sent home early from Mary's party, I'm going to tend to you.' Within half an hour after he left, Johnny returned with a scowl on his face. His mother was furious and sent him up to his room to wait her coming. When she had cooled off a little, she climbed the stairs and entered.

" ' Johnny, tell me the truth now. Why did Mrs. Jones send you home? Can't you act nicely just once? ' ' Aw, gee, Maw,' said Johnny, ' you're always blaming me. That dopey old party was yesterday! ' "

When differences occur at home, there are proved ways of handling them. One way (and this is not facetious) is to ignore them. Many a quarrel between family members is of such insignificant nature that there is true wisdom in letting them " fight it out." To intervene in every instance of bickering is likely to shut off some wholesome expression of hostility and may work an injustice in the bargain.

Another way that enjoys the sanctity of time-honored practice is the talk-it-over session. In the family council it is possible to get off one's chest the complaints that one feels, and also to take everyone into the planning process for family decisions. This step alone prevents untold dissension. It may even stop the plaintive, " No one ever consults me about anything."

" A word fitly spoken," says the writer of The Proverbs, " is like apples of gold in pictures of silver." Certainly a word of encouragement can be an extremely valuable thing. Praise carries the weight of ten scoldings. It brings a grateful response that far exceeds any value a criticism might evoke. A few years back, the Western Electric Company conducted a series of experiments in employee relations to learn how best to increase efficiency. Although they tried refreshments, rest periods, entertainment, and other favors, they found that the highest degree of efficiency came *in response to encouragement*. It works in households too.

Whistle While You Work

Disagreement can be aroused easily in families; but you can find it still faster by assigning a work detail. Complaints from sister that she must do more than anyone else are offset by groans from brother that he never gets to do anything but work.

Parents will find that the members of the family are more disposed to whistle while they work if a few basic principles are adopted:

1. Adults must set the working example. Lazy children just might be chips off the old block.

2. Let each person have some choice in what he would like to do. There are limits to the choices, of course. But most of us are happier in our tasks when they are self-assigned.

3. Don't overwork the youngsters. This one is tricky because it is difficult to establish the golden mean between indolence and compulsory servitude.

4. Accentuate the positive side of work. Show how it serves the family. When scheduling the jobs, put it this way: "Today we will mow the lawn and clean the basement. Where would you rather work?"

5. Be specific about the job but allow wide leeway in how it gets done. This makes the worker responsible for completing the work in his own way without interference.

Learning to love work is a slow process, and most of us never quite attain this goal. Sharing in the duties of the household, however, is a step in the right direction. Washing the dishes or polishing the car can be just as dull for young people as for adults. But the youngsters have a valuable lesson when they realize this fact. Their willingness to help in household responsibilities is increased when they feel that they have a real stake in the family, when they know their efforts will be noticed and appreciated, and when they recognize that others in the family are also pulling their share of the load.

From father's first surprised look at his wrinkled infant to the day that his grandchildren are brought home for a visit, the youngsters seem never to be quite what he had expected. Years of training are spent in trying to change these children of ours into something better. In this exacting task most parents do a respectable job, but they are bound to feel the heavy hand of failure somewhere along the line.

Mistakes are rife in this business of family living. "It doesn't need a war to flatten things," says a character in a novel by Graham Greene. ". . . Parents . . . are just as good as war." It is sobering to realize how much damage parents can do. Until rather recently, however, there has been too much emphasis on this danger. Inevitably, parents have been made to feel demoralized and guilty; and the churches have at times increased this sense of guilt among Christian families. But most fathers and mothers conscientiously rear their families. They need guidance more than they need criticism.

In the process of child training, parents learn a lot themselves. They come to see that co-operation is a two-way street, that generosity and honest attempts at understanding are astonishingly practical in family relations, and that counseling and earnest talks are best received if given in terms of love.

Quarrels are normal in every household. Hostility and aggression find expression in every individual. Exasperating tensions are found " in the best of families." The solution lies not in trying to erase every one of these all-too-natural feelings, but in learning to cope with them. In this program, there is just no substitute for Christian love.

3: DISCIPLINE
IN THE CHRISTIAN HOME

Mother said to him, "You must do as I tell you." He replied, "Why should I?" The mother found it difficult, but she said, "You must do what I tell you because I have had to do what my mother told me, and she had to do what her mother told her." "H'm," said John, "I wonder who started that silly game."
— *Leslie Weatherhead, in* Psychology and Life.

THERE is a mistaken notion prevailing among some parents that discipline is the same thing as punishment. It is not. Discipline comes from a Latin word meaning "to teach." The best discipline is that which teaches, not the kind that hurts. When handled well, our discipline is dispensed with love. To put it another way, love is in itself the best form of discipline. This means that discipline is never correctly applied when its source is parental convenience or parental annoyance. Wise parents understand that growing up is a slow, sometimes painful, process. All discipline, therefore, must be accompanied by patience. After all, its ultimate goal is self-mastery in the child, and not regulation or regimentation by some older person. Parents must understand that discipline means much more than management of children. Indeed, it means that they must grow in learning how to think for themselves and in ruling themselves.

Wise fathers and mothers recognize that there must be rules in the home. If the child is to survive, he must know the rules of safety. If he is to be well, he must be taught the rules of health. If he is to be socially acceptable in the homes of friends, he must be taught the rules of courtesy. A child actually appreciates the standards the older generation teaches him if by means of them he can govern his actions. Without them, he feels insecure and lost. Most children readily recognize guidance and (somewhat less readily) accept it. But they are also keen in spotting those rules which have been laid down in order to cover up the boredom, or self-interest, or weaknesses of adults. The wisdom of little children is often a remarkable thing and their discernment in such situations is sometimes acute.

The Christian parent is not without standards for this exacting task. More than others, he should recognize that the child is precious also in the eyes of God, and that even "one of these little ones" deserves the most considerate treatment. Alas, however, not all church homes have consistent Christian dealings among family members, and discipline is one place where the breakdown is most easily seen.

Children actually appreciate firmness. They may not always show their appreciation; indeed, they may show their annoyance instead. Yet deep down underneath they like to know that there are some principles on which they can lean, even if their choice would not always favor firm principles. The young child honestly likes to feel that there is a parent who will prevent him from being naughty when he is unable to govern himself. The teen-ager, however much it may seem otherwise, really likes to know that there are definite standards about the places he may go and the things he may be allowed to do, even though he seems to wish that all life were anarchy so that he could ignore the laws for himself. Children themselves sometimes ask for firmer rules. Children of Harlem in New York City were questioned a few years ago about their feelings concerning authority, and, believe it or not, they voted that they should have more whippings!

Somewhat typical is the experience of the child who had spent a troubled day, getting into one difficulty after another. The mother was unable to control him, and had all but given up when the child cried, " Oh, when is my daddy going to come home and *make* me behave? " Children really like controls because they sometimes fear what they may do if they are not stopped from harmful acts.

Boys and girls soon learn whether discipline is consistent. If parents cannot agree about it, then their disagreement is soon discovered and exploited by sons and daughters who know how to play one off against the other. What is sometimes worse, the child can be torn between the conflicting directions of his father and mother, unsure of what is really right, and fearful of angry intervention if he obeys one in disagreement with the other.

All children need to recognize authority in their parents. A feeling of security and of confidence accrues from the recognition that even if a child wavers in decision between right and wrong, his dad can point it out. Sometimes, to our surprise, this elicits a grateful response from the little one who somehow couldn't stop being naughty but was checked by Dad, or the teen-ager who would waver about his curfew time except for an insistence upon eleven o'clock from Mother. That father has missed the point who supposes that " to be a buddy " means that he should avoid imposing his will when necessary. For children actually look to their dads for protection and guidance, because their dads happen to be stronger and more experienced.

This is not to say, however, that Dad can use his authority as father only through a vulgar display of power. The best kind of discipline is that which hurts the least. Although pain is an aid to learning, satisfaction is more potent. The sort of strictness that leaves a youngster hurt and humiliated can win the point, but it is an empty victory.

Discipline defeats its own purpose if it quells the youngster's ability to form his own decisions. Lest he go through life always looking to Father for orders, it is better to train him to control himself, even at the cost of his making some mistakes of his own.

Recent research indicates a trend away from the traditional concept of father (the patriarch whose word is law and whose authority dare not be questioned) toward what the sociologists call the developmental concept. By the same token we are spared hearing, "Mother knows best," as frequently as it was once dinned upon tender ears. The developmental concept of parent-child relations instead takes into acount the need for self-expression in the child, and the greater effectiveness of the parent who explains and works things out with his children. This kind of parent does not fear to admit when he is wrong, nor does he punish in order to cover up his own error. Instead, he loves his children enough to see them as persons in their own right, never to be treated as personal possessions.

Even when it is necessary to discipline a child overtly and firmly, the wise adult makes it clear that his displeasure with wrong conduct does not lessen his love for the child. An injury is done to the child who feels that he is rejected because he has been taken to task.

And this in its finite way is an insight into the ways in which God regards those created in his image. Loving us in spite of our sin, permitting us the option of choosing or rejecting his grace, he never violates us as persons. Rather he leads us, finds us again when we have strayed, and forgives us when we err.

In all of the disciplining of children, it is necessary for parents to know their own minds, and to keep their own self-control. The parent who flies off the handle and corrects a child in anger has lost from the situation the teaching values that otherwise would have been present.

Parents must remember that a child's total behavior pattern has to be considered in any kind of discipline. For instance, his simple muscular actions are far different from those of adults. His mental reasoning is only slightly similar to adult reasoning. Because of these factors, the child is prone to make mistakes of judgment and to misgauge his actions. The pitcher of milk on the table seems to Father to be a trifling problem, easily passed from hand to hand when care is taken. But to the three-year-old child whose chin barely clears the surface of the table, the pitcher looks twice as big as to the adult, and to his smaller hands it is certainly twice the problem in manipulation. Yet, when he spills the pitcher of milk, he is likely to be confronted with some growl like: " Now, see what you've done! Why can't you be more careful? "

It aids the discipline of children if parents can remember to keep themselves in check, recalling constantly that a child's thinking and his connection of past and future events are altogether different from that of adults. This makes him less able to learn from experience, and less adept at planning for the next experience. To accept the child as the person he is, at the stage of development where he stands, is to know him better and get along better with him. Living in a Christian home must mean that each person is loved and respected for his own sake.

It is well also for parents to remember that when disputes arise they should bear no resentment nor show any enmity to the child after the issue is past. The child who feels that he has been shut out or is now unloved suffers more than grownups ever realize. His feeling of not being wanted is perhaps the most dangerous impression possible on his young mind. Forgiveness must always play its part in family living.

Forcing a child into obedience is a risky form of discipline. Unless a child learns to obey the common-sense rules of life without being forced into them, he can hardly grow strong enough in his own character to take care of himself. Wise discipline, therefore, requires that the child be taught to think and act for himself. It takes a mature parent to discipline a child. To take advantage of a child's younger years and his inexperience can be a vile and unkind thing, unless it also guides him in his living. Moreover, physical discipline soon becomes self-defeating when Junior grows too large to spank, and no other persuasion so far has worked.

The actual clashes that come from discipline are often trivial in nature. But they can loom disproportionately important in relationships. Generations ago, when father and son worked side by side in the fields from sunrise to sundown, any conflict between them could be worked off before the call to noon meal. Nowadays, if a dad and his lad have a falling-out at 8 o'clock (it may be the only time in the entire day they are together), all their day's experiences can be colored by this incident.

Is Punishment Ever Justified?

What many parents only half realize is that the nagging, lashing tongue is perhaps the worst punishment that can be administered to children. The cartoon from a *Saturday Evening Post* showing a mother and father leaving their son for the day is instructive. In her parting directions, the mother says to the sitter, " Every ten minutes put your head out of the back door and yell: ' No, no, Junior, don't do that! ' " Children themselves have testified that the tongue-lashing they received from their parents can make them ill. In some ways it can be worse than a spanking, and the sting can be more lasting.

Punishment is negative and only temporary in its effectiveness. It stops the child in some action of his without giving him a correlative, positive suggestion. Punishment frustrates. Although it may take care of immediate and temporary situations, punishment rarely is good discipline. Often it has arisen from a situation in which the parents are irritated or tired. Then the child may be bewildered on finding that the selfsame act that brought approval yesterday may bring penalty today. It is this inconsistent character of punishment that makes it so dangerous to use.

As Helen Parkhurst has explained in the book *Exploring the Child's World:* " If it relieves parents' pent-up feelings, it is a selfish thing at the expense of the child. . . . Punishment strikes terror in the child's heart and makes him fearful of another person, perhaps the most important being in his life, a parent, someone he loves."

Ironically a vast amount of punishment comes from the good intentions of parents. They feel that they are indulging in the practice in order to train their child to be a better person. In reality, however, they fail to take account of the personhood of the child they are punishing, and that the improvement they hope to achieve may actually be blocked by their method. Many years ago, Reverend John Skelton wrote a poem called " Magnificence." In it there were two memorable lines:

> " There is nothing that more displeaseth God,
> Than from their children to spare the rod."

From these two rhyming lines has come one of the poorest of all slogans in child training, namely, " Spare the rod and spoil the child." Yet many parents feel that they are doing a good job of child training if they punish frequently. By this mistaken theory parents can degrade, humiliate, and discourage their own family.

A child speaks out, " I think if the parents have reasons for their punishment, then the children would try to correct their wrongs." However, if children are punished simply without explanation, their attitude toward the wrong they have committed remains essentially unchanged. This obviously is not discipline as we have defined it. Perhaps the main difficulty with punishment is that like the quick cure in medicine, it treats only the superficial symptoms and does not reach the basic underlying disease. The deeper question is what has caused the misbehavior in the first place. When this problem is met, we can better understand how to handle the matter of correction. It may truly be said that the parent who punishes often is actually evading the major job of discipline. He stands a good chance of defeating his own purpose. You can almost score yourself — the frequency of punishment is inversely proportionate to your skill in discipline, according to Sidonie Gruenberg, author of *Your Child and You*. She goes on to write: "Home is the place a child must be helped to learn from his mistakes, not to be forced to suffer from them. No parent would think of letting his child go all winter without a warm coat because he had lost his." Nor should we compel children always to suffer for their mistakes by making them the victims of their own inexperience.

It was an old Dutch maxim that a blow at the bottom lets in knowledge at the top. This method of child training, however, is under considerable suspicion these days. Especially those methods of corporal punishment that have to do with slapping children or knocking them about the head and ears are held to be downright dangerous and injurious. Even spankings have come under considerable criticism, not so much because they harm a child as that they are of no proved value.

So too the parent who punishes by assigning additional chores around the house, or by denying the child access to a meal, or by sending him to bed can make a mistake in confusing some of the commonplace habits and privileges of household living with punishment. The result may be that he makes these ordinary duties and customs to be disagreeable. They may even remain distasteful to the child for long years to come. The same parents may subsequently complain because the child refuses to eat, or will not go to bed, or will not happily do tasks around the house.

Punishment certainly carries with it an unfortunate amount of additional burden. A child who is punished too often, especially by physical means, learns to resort to lying and cheating in order to avoid chastisement. The mother or father who continues to harp on bygones is keeping alive feelings of inferiority and hostility in a child. The parent who puts a special emphasis upon confession, saying in effect, " If you will tell the truth, you will not be punished," does so at the considerable risk of making the act of confession seem more important than the original incident. Punishment may prove to be self-defeating.

There are many wrong ways to punish a child. Perhaps the worst of them are those measures which use inconsiderate and unfair methods. The father or mother who in anger breathes terrible threats to the child often regrets it later on. To say, " You will have no allowance for six weeks," is arranging a condition the parent may soon find as uncomfortable as does the child. To be true to this word will necessitate sticking by an extravagant threat.

Seldom has the nature of parental tyranny been described as well as George Santayana put it in his recent book, *Dominations and Powers*. For this bachelor-philosopher had somehow captured the mixture of deep love and authoritarianism that a parent exhibits toward his child.

" Parents necessarily exercise authority over their young children . . . becoming in this way veritable tyrants. But tyrants are seldom free; the cares and the instruments of their tyranny enslave them. The child that cries is your master; and he is your master again when he smiles. . . . Nature kindly warps our judgment about children, especially when they are young, when it would be a fatal thing for them if we did not love them. This fond blindness is itself a slavery; a hard slavery, when you think of it, to feel a compulsory and sleepless affection . . . and afterwards to be disgraced by his disgrace, wounded by his indifference, and half killed by his death, if you survive him."

It was Rabindranath Tagore who said, "He only may chastise who loves." Certainly, discipline is best handled under conditions of love, for it is when the disciplinary action is prompted by a real interest in the personality of the child that it is really effective. Their growth, their character, their independence are to be considered in the disciplinary process. It is far more important to contribute to these than to eliminate the annoyance of a fleeting moment.

Certainly when love is withdrawn in discipline or when there is some threat of its being withdrawn through such an idiotic sentence as, "Mother won't love you if you don't stop doing that," or, "I'm going to get me a new little boy," the harm exceeds any possible value. John Baillie tells in his *Invitation to Pilgrimage* that as a boy he recognized that the authority his father exercised in the home was really subject in turn to the higher authority of God. His father thus used his position responsibly, even reverently, and at the same time taught something to his son about the sovereignty of God.

Discipline Is for Parents

In the main, discipline of children must be thought of more as an objective for parents than for the children themselves. What does this mean but that an example of self-discipline on the part of parents is better by far than any direct scolding of the child? The paramount goal of the parent is to learn to control himself; and this is particularly necessary when the child is most aggravating.

Good behavior, something that every parent wants in his children, is the result of an *inner willingness,* not of outer compulsion. The best type of discipline does not come by means of a rod; for the rod does not bring long-lasting effects of good behavior. Permitting a child to express his own freedom and action, and also to bear his own consequences in error and petty frustrations is good teaching. In the long run discipline is a reasoning process wherein example is highly important. It is possible for children to be punished without ever having been truly disciplined. Anyhow, good discipline is found generally alongside of happiness. Pleasurable and secure feelings in the child's mind do more for good behavior than almost any amount of corporal punishment or force. And in the end it certainly means that a home is happier.

Well-adjusted children are those who have been wisely taught at home. Theirs are the parents who have made of discipline a wholesome, positive relationship. According to Dr. Alexander Reid Martin, director of the Children's Aid Society in New York City, parents of this type have these half dozen characteristics: (1) they listen to and accept the child's early ambitions, (2) they do things with the child and not just for him, (3) they tell stories to children, (4) they laugh and joke with children, (5) they do things together as a family, (6) they give their children real jobs to do in the home.

In the long run, it is not the mistakes in the handling of a child that stand out in his memory or that determine his life so much as it is the total climate of the home. A wholesome amount of real affection is far more important than the outward indications of the parent-child relationship. Yes, it is even possible that a father who uses improper and physical measures in dealing with his child in the long run still can be a successful parent. But this happens when the over-all degree of love in the home is so full and so evident to the child that it outweighs whatever mistakes the parent makes in times of anger, or of fatigue, or of ignorance.

Obviously, this cannot mean that the parent who fondles his child is making up for harsh treatment. Love cannot be interpreted in this instance as mere hugging and kissing. It is something that goes far deeper into the way that the child finds companionship, guidance, and support from his parents.

Spurgeon English, in *Fathers Are Parents, Too,* writes:

" The whole matter of discipline is nicely summed up quite unintentionally by a father who said: ' I'm away from home so much that I just don't have a chance to discipline my children. When I'm around I just have fun with them. They tell me about what they've been doing and I talk about some of the things I've done and seen. Sometimes we discuss some of the things we think are pretty important to having a good life and being useful and happy. I don't get time to scold or punish them, but for some reason they don't need it. They're pretty good kids on the whole and I tell them so. Then they hug me and my wife says our home is a mutual admiration society. If that's so, then admiration seems to work! ' "

Needless to say, this parent had blundered into the finest of disciplinary techniques. He was treating his children as real persons; and they were responding in a perfectly predictable way. It is one of the strangest contradictions in life that people who are convinced that Christianity must be operative in the world at large sometimes fail to see its relevance to homes. Yet, if the faith is to be practiced anywhere it must begin in families. In the words of Paul, " let them learn first to show piety at home."

4: PARENTS VERSUS FAMILY FINANCES

More and more parents are making intelligent use of an "allowance" as an effective instrument for educating the child about money through his personal experience with it. They are learning to "give" a child his own money just as they give him oatmeal or an overcoat, without irrelevant emotion and without using their power over the purse strings to coerce or bribe him to do the "right" thing.

— *Sidonie Matsner Gruenberg, in* Our Children Today.

SOME parents, we are given to understand, have an embarrassment of riches and are baffled about how to manage and spend their large sums of money. The vast majority of families, however, are seldom bothered by this quandary. Theirs is quite a different problem. In the average home such funds as are available must somehow stretch over the many categories of expense and obligation: beans and beanies, telephones and taxes, benevolences and books, tables and television, and a host of other important items that challenge the family exchequer. Families with children are seldom puzzled by any accumulation of financial surplus.

Yet the ever-present conundrum of how to stretch income over outgo is not the only subject of family financing. Parents know other questions:

How shall we teach our children to use money — and not let it use them?

What can we do to help our family to understand the claims of Christian stewardship — that what we are and what we have should always be used in the service of God?

Children learn about money by having money to use. It's as simple as that. They learn how to use a hammer by pounding nails, or they catch on to balancing a bicycle through the experience of riding one.

This means that some way must be devised to allow children the use of a regular, limited sum, such as an allowance makes possible. The question of what age a child should be when he first receives an allowance is not easily answered. Although this decision must depend upon individual considerations, one general observation can be made — most parents do not put children on an allowance soon enough. Your child is ready when he knows how to count, when he exhibits a consistent need of money for purchases, when he shows an interest in money, or when he has some understanding of the needs of other people.

The proved method is to start a child with an allowance of a few pennies, and then to increase the amount gradually each birthday or with new requirements such as cub scout dues or extra school expenses.

To the objection that our four-, five-, or six-year-olds are too young to know a nickel from a dime, the answer is easy: they soon learn when they have the opportunity. Interestingly, some parents report that when they placed their children on the allowance system, it resulted in less instead of more handouts. The dole gets more expensive because it is frequently demanded and is unsystematic.

What is more, it teaches almost nothing except how to make a soft touch on Dad.

Henry C. Link in his last book, *The Way to Security*, stated a dark opinion about the allowance system: " The theory of the automatic, unearned allowance for children is one of the greatest disservices ever perpetrated on education and the American people." Nor is this all. Convinced that unearned allowances delay maturity and that weaker personalities result, Mr. Link poured scorn upon grants of money that are unrelated to payment for jobs accomplished.

This does emphasize a good point — that children can grow in responsibility if they perform remunerative work. The point, however, can be overdrawn. The objective in granting an allowance is to teach youngsters the use of money, a necessary skill in our civilization. It also helps them to realize how they share in the welfare of the family. There are certain dangers in permitting the allowance to be tied to whatever jobs are accomplished. Sooner or later every favor may seem to have its own price tag if this practice is carried too far.

The assigning of jobs and the arrangement of wages, therefore, must be judiciously handled. Fictional tasks that do no good but simply require the motions are meaningless. The labor ought to be of such nature that it actually benefits the household. Lawn mowing, car washing, and house cleaning are some of the usual jobs. Payment for these tasks must be somewhat arbitrary, and custom must be fitted to the individual. There is a more powerful influence on the child's desire to work than the pay he receives to do it. As we noted in Chapter 2, observing the spirit of the parents as they go about their tasks is the key to how well the younger generation learns to work.

Part-time work is valuable for teen-agers. Earning money in employment outside the home helps them to understand what money costs. The question of whether the teen-ager contributes to family expenses should be carefully considered according to a group of facts, such as the need of the family, the amount of the earnings, and the savings plan involved.

In money matters, as in other family issues, the example of the parents is decisive. The way in which they handle their own money, their regard for it, and their habits about financial worries will make the difference. Fathers and mothers are generally unaware of the many patterns regarding money that are directly passed on to the children. Doubtless these patterns were established before the children were born. Money habits may be cemented by the honeymoon if not before.

The spending picture must be a puzzle to the young child. He sees his mother give money to utter strangers for little packages. And sometimes they return what appears to be even more money to her. At other times she gives money to the bus driver, who evidently gives no parcel in return. One description of a child's impressions of money found in *Money Management: Children's Spending* reads thus:

" References to money popped up all over Jimmy's small world, and slowly but surely he collected an odd and unrelated set of facts and fancies. He learned that money doesn't grow on trees. . . . He heard that a ten-dollar bill simply melts away and that money has a way of slipping through fingers or burning holes in pockets. He wasn't willing to accept the fact that money talks, however, because he had spent many odd moments questioning both the paper and silver variety without getting so much as one word in response. . . .

" Suddenly he wondered whether anyone would object to his

taking money which they had poured down ratholes. But where was a rathole?

"The shadow of money hung over Jimmy's very playmates. Alice, Grandmother said, had been born with a silver spoon in her mouth. . . . Maryanne, whose mother was poor as a church mouse, was considered a darling, and Billy was pitied because his family lived 'over their heads.' Jimmy spent every minute he could spare from playing to watch for penny pinchers, spendthrifts, and squanderlusts. Whenever he happened to have a penny of his own, he would clutch it very tightly, remembering the words Aunt Emma was forever saying so darkly, 'A fool and his money are soon parted.'"

We forget too soon how complex the adult world is to the child, how confusing our manner of speech. Lucky is that youngster whose parents carefully teach him about money, explaining strange matters to him, and giving practical opportunities through a systematic allowance to learn more.

The wise parent does not link money to the discipline of children. Virtue cannot be bribed by a bonus allowance or a special grant. Nor does the withholding of funds really take care of behavior problems. To refuse allowance to a child because he has been naughty makes as much sense as a man's cutting down on the household budget because he is temporarily displeased with his wife. Only confused thinking about the purpose of money makes possible the linking of allowance to discipline. A fuller discussion of the issue of discipline and allowances is found in Chapter 3.

When problems do arise in regard to children's spending, as they sometimes will, these problems can be dealt with individually. The buying of improperly balanced lunches, for instance, is a nutritional matter. Conspicuous spending to impress the gang is less a financial than an emotional question. A boy whose buying sprees collect useless articles may be attempting to compensate for some deeper need of which he is only vaguely aware. Instead of cutting off his allowance, the parents should trace that need.

Parents should not be alarmed if the child with an allowance spends his money foolishly at times. Some momentary reflection will remind them that they squander occasionally too. When he does squander all his allowance at once, and is penniless for the remainder of the week, the kind parent helps to pull him out of this difficulty once or twice, rather than permitting him to flounder. The ability to understand money and to spend it wisely does not come to a child suddenly. Over the years this dawns on him with experience.

Bribery has no place in the financial arrangements of the home. To promise Johnny a dollar if he plays well in the piano recital is not the proper approach. But if Johnny plays well, a reward may be in order: " Johnny, you were splendid in the recital tonight. Can't you use an extra dollar in your jeans? "

The parent should not expect too much from the discrimination of a child. Buying skills are learned only gradually — witness any young bride. If the family is on a trip, the treats can be supplied by parents. If the allowance has run out early in the week, detours should be made around those tempting counters of the five-and-ten-cent store until the sum can be replenished.

If modern parents are to interpret the wise use of money to their little ones, they will have to know what their own attitude is. They may be forced to do a substantial job of rethinking the entire question for their children will witness their family's handling of money and will be influenced by it.

Typical stages in the growth and use of money can be found in the chart presented in this chapter (see pages 58 and 59). Individual children may arrive at such development earlier or later than the examples designate, yet though these gradations cannot be accurate for each case they illustrate how money educates through experience.

Freedom Helps to Educate

If Junior is ever to learn money management, he must have enough freedom to make some mistakes. True, he may squander his entire week's allowance on some unwise purchase; he may be fleeced of some amount by a slick companion; he may even lose it while playing.

To place excessive restrictions upon the child's spending, however, is to reduce his opportunities to learn by experience. The process of learning to spend wisely has to involve the appreciation of how slowly money comes in and how rapidly it is gone. Experience also teaches how change is made, what prices are, how loans are negotiated (usually with Dad), and what it means to give to good causes. This same permissive arrangement allows leeway for a lad to change his mind in the midst of a savings project, switching from his plan for a trip to the more immediate goal of a new football.

Only through a liberal program that permits freedom of choices in spending and saving is the control of money learned. Rules imposed upon the child by his elders about how the money is to be spent, what portion is to be saved, and similar regulations, have little place in this educational venture. It must be a spend-as-you-please allowance, no matter how small it is or how tight the family funds. Through the years, then, the amount of the allowance can be gradually increased as the child's responsibilities and judgment increase.

" The best things in life are free " runs the refrain of a popular song. It is one way of saying that there are some invaluable privileges that money cannot buy. It cannot replace all the breakage a boy may perpetrate. The shattered windowpane, yes. The antique vase and heirloom, no. It cannot purchase good feelings when a prized rose has been trampled in play; nor can it grow a new bloom.

Even the youngest soon learn that small sums cannot buy numerous coveted articles. Elenore T. Pounds, writing in *Parents' Magazine,* tells of her four-year-old daughter, who learned the hard facts of prices when she spied something she wanted. She would hold out her few pennies in hand to the clerk, asking, " Is this enough? " If it was not, she would accept without rancor the clerk's reply. Gradually a knowledge of money's limitations led her to a self-instituted savings program, so that she could accumulate enough for desired purchases. In time she became a canny shopper, comparing prices, and often walking out without making purchases at all. To know money's limitations, indeed, is to know one of the most significant facts about it. America is well-populated with people who erroneously think that money is power, or that money means success.

As the child grows older, both his abilities and his responsibilities increase. So also his share of the family funds increases. Now comes the time when the girl or boy buys some of his own clothing. Oh, what choices these can be! Although there is certain learning value in making a horrible choice and having to live with it, the purple shirt

GROWTH AND USE OF MONEY
FROM AGES 4 TO 18

AGE	THE ALLOWANCE	HOUSEHOLD AND OTHER JOBS	GIVING AND TITHING
Age 4	Some children are ready for a weekly allowance.	Does simple house tasks: setting table, picking up toys.	Takes money to nursery class. Participates in simple gifts to family.
Age 5	Can intelligently use 5 to 10 cents a week.	Begins emptying wastebaskets, dusting, caring for own room.	Continues with gifts at kindergarten. Grows aware of needy people. Develops generosity.
Age 6	Persistent needs at school, store, and in gang already prompt demands for raise.	Can be paid for vacuuming rugs, raking leaves, making beds.	Is erratically generous and miserly. Sees new horizons of giving: missions, polio fund, Christmas.
Age 7	Ability to go into stores alone and to count change deserves a regular allowance.	Is genuinely able to perform useful tasks for remuneration — errands, house cleaning, care of younger sister or brother.	Can tithe his own money now. Youth Budget Plan at Sunday church school may include this age.
Age 8	Allowance can now be in two parts: basic amount given by parents, and earned amount that varies but augments this basic amount.	Occasionally works for neighbors, running errands, helping to clean garage.	Grows more interested in causes that are interpreted to him at school and church.
Age 9	Begins to see personal allowance in proportion to family finances. Now able to take part in minor decisions on family budget.	Continues in simple tasks for family and neighbors.	Awakens more and more to the claims on his charity. Is responsive when these are interpreted to him.

Age 10	By now should have a savings account in which regular sums are deposited.	Branches into new fields of earning – selling Christmas cards and magazine subscriptions.	Should be able to participate in family discussions about tithing and charity.
Age 11	Able to keep simple accounts in a personal budget book. Expanding activities require larger sums.	Baby-sits during daytime, sweeps or shovels off walks, tends furnace.	Is alert to special gifts for friends. Occasionally arranges collections for projects.
Age 12	Maturing judgment now can be trusted in certain purchases of clothing. (Another raise indicated!)	Scouts, parties, and hobbies need more support; so he asks more for doing jobs and should receive more if the service warrants.	Is now old enough to help in financial drives and deliberations of church group.
Age 13	Realistic arrangement in family council essential to establish agreement in tug between enlarging activities and family exchequer.	Delivers newspapers, gardens, baby-sits. Is capable, if not always willing, to do nearly all sorts of family tasks, e.g., cooking, ironing, repairing, painting.	Finds more responsible positions in Red Cross, Youth Budget, foreign aid, clothing collections.
Ages 14–16	Getting into dating period now opens up new costs. Few families can afford the size of allowance a teen-ager wishes. Supplement it with earnings.	By 16, young people are employable in part-time jobs in drugstores, groceries, offices, on farms.	Is able to give more generously from additional work income. Tithing an excellent system.
Ages 17, 18	This age can receive entire clothes allowance to spend at discretion. Should be apprised of family obligations so as to take a mature part in co-operative planning.	Occasional temptations to quit school for paying jobs must be dealt with. Though nearing young adult age, the 18-year-old still needs counsel.	Contributions to the family from earnings need now to be considered, and training of earlier years now shows through.

or the skirt with diagonal stripes can also have a demoralizing effect. It is well to allow those first clothing purchases to be pajamas. If they are outlandish mistakes, at least the eyes that see them are few. With time, the number and scope of clothing purchases can be increased as more is learned about these choices.

In that charming play, *I Remember Mama,* Mama calls the entire family together when Papa brings home his pay check. She then distributes it to food, rent, school supplies, clothes; and the family discuss what they can do to make it reach yet farther. Then Mama sums it up in her winsome Scandinavian dialect: " Is good that children learn about money in this way."

Truly, money presents a family project. In a sense, all their income is family income, all their expense family expense. The family budget calls for a togetherness of spirit and of action. This can be reached through the accord of a family council.

By the time Junior is in high school he can be included in the family budget sessions so that he also understands how it works, how much is involved, and where the money goes. When the parents show this much confidence, their young people will likely respond by being understanding and discreet.

The idea of the family council in budgetary decisions is not different from that in other deliberations. Such a council gives an opportunity for all members of the family group to talk over their finances, to discuss the needs of each person and the amounts that can be allotted for those needs, and to share the heavy responsibilities involved. Because the wage earner alone cannot settle so complex an issue as the financial budget for the home, he calls in all the others who are involved. Here in council the rules are discussed, amounts are set, charge accounts are examined, and privileges concerning them are granted.

The discussion is in terms of "our money," in the collective outlook of a close-knit family drawn together in this democratic act. Children learn in council what money can and cannot do, and by this lesson in democracy they also find that their parents are not using money to gain control over them. The parents do well to consider the ages and the discretion of their children as they work out monetary problems. With younger children, it may be wiser to introduce financial subjects only with minor decisions, and with infrequent inclusion of the amounts mentioned. This prevents enthusiastic juveniles from talking too freely of family affairs.

In the homes where such a measure has been inaugurated, fathers and mothers have evinced surprise at the understanding shown by the children. They come through with helpful suggestions on economy, allowances, and budget. All the while, they are enrolled in a very practical course in economics, learning how the family can spend, save, and share.

Making Ends Meet Is Difficult

Poor Mr. Micawber, that stanch friend of David Copperfield, has become the regular example of the man with budget troubles. Of his home, Mr. Micawber said: "The only visitors were creditors. They used to come at all hours, and some of them were quite ferocious."

The ferocious character of home finances is altogether too well known to the modern family. Our inflationary spiral in post World War II years sharply increased the cost of automobile fenders, hamburger, tricycles, and blue jeans. Many a family, as a result, feels the constant nagging of financial worry and that bothersome concern over meeting the next installment on what was evidently humorously entitled an " easy payment plan."

In these circumstances it takes a surprisingly short time to run up a series of mountainous debts. The debts can be followed by still more family tensions, as attempts are made to meet obligations. Doubtless some family groups feel more strain than others; the same kind of crisis often brings a quite different reaction in a neighboring home.

The dollar bill has sometimes been called " Home Maker or Breaker Number One." It is true that arguments arise quickly between husband and wife if there is misunderstanding about money. A court judge has reported: " Quarreling about money is a major reason for America's unprecedented divorce rate. It is difficult to overestimate the vicious part financial trouble is playing in the American home." In one study it was discovered that young husbands attributed forty-eight per cent of their most serious marital problems to financial difficulties. When either deflation or inflation makes it more difficult to stretch the money over all the household necessities, the tendency to find fault and to bicker becomes the greater.

In recent years we have been confronted with increased taxes, caused in part by the Government's armament program. When to nationally caused problems there is sometimes added a health difficulty in the family that requires special diet or hospitalization, or when there is an additional obligation to support an aged parent, the financial crisis can become nearly unmanageable.

Young adults who are just beginning married life face particular financial problems. It is likely that they will continue to be on the move, seeking better employment across the nation, or sometimes living near Army camps. Young families may be forced to dwell in makeshift homes because with rising costs and nearly static incomes they cannot always afford the standard of living they would prefer. Savings and insurance plans, like the fond hope of entering a business for oneself, must be adjusted or postponed. Parents of young couples today are finding it necessary to subsidize their married children — that is, if the parents themselves can afford it.

Although it is a scare word in political circles, a " planned " economy is just what the family needs. Not even the very rich dare to spend money without caring what happens to it. Yet many families seem never to know where their pay check has gone. Particularly when prices are high and wages limited, the family income needs to be planned carefully in personal finance management. Planned spending, of course, means budgeting. But it does not mean the sort of inflexible system that becomes a tyrant rather than a servant to the family. The important thing to keep in mind is that the budget was built for the family, and not the family for the budget. The process need not be complicated.

J. K. Lasser and Sylvia F. Porter outline just four basic steps of planning a budget in their book *How to Live Within Your Income*. These steps are:

1. Figure accurately your annual income. Then arrange this sum in twelve monthly portions.

2. Analyze your big fixed expenses of the year, and your savings. This includes insurance premiums, taxes, and debt payments.

3. Deduct the amount that remains from these fixed expenses. This is for day-to-day expenditures.

4. Now plan these day-to-day living expenses carefully.

(Unless this information is written down, the budget cannot be said to be entirely useful.) Something better is needed than the system of the young bride who summarized one month as, " March 1, Jim gave me $100 "; then, on the opposite page, " March 31, spent it all."

The sharing of financial responsibility by all the family brings the most co-operation. Today less than formerly we hear about the marriages in which one partner handles all the money and the other is completely ignorant of the income and expenses. But this species is not extinct, by any means. And of all patterns of family spending, this is probably the poorest. Imagine, if you can, a business partnership in which one half of the firm does not know the source of the income. Yet a marriage is a closer relationship than is any business partnership.

The family can cope with skyrocketing expenses only if they plan their use of all the money *and stick to the plan.* This will require occasional auditing of the accounts to make sure that some one item is not claiming more of the budget than it should. It is not unusual for a budget to get out of control because of disproportionate spending.

Mark Twain's annual new year's resolution resembles the system of many of us. He used to pledge: " This year I shall live within my income even if I must borrow the money to do it." The specter of debt looms over the chimneys of many homes. Borrowing money in order to live within a proposed income is sadly frequent.

The debts pile up in many ways: bank loans, " touching " personal friends, buying overmuch on charge accounts, or taking on major obligations in installment purchases. (Installment buying is sometimes called the glad-and-sorry system — glad that you have the article, sorry that you must pay so many months for it.) Perhaps no one else has so well expressed the frustration of the installment buyer as Willy Loman in the play *Death of a Salesman:*

" Once in my life I would like to own something outright before it's broken! I'm always in a race with the junk yard! I just finished paying for the car and it's on its last legs. The refrigerator consumes belts like a . . . maniac. They time those things. They time them so when you've finally paid for them, they're used up."

Yet there are ways of avoiding entanglements with one's money. To prevent it from controlling our whole lives we must learn two lessons: to economize and to keep our Christian sense of values.

Experience has taught families to find the corners that can be cut in their particular homes in order to avoid financial troubles. Some of the most widely accepted methods are these:

1. *Lay aside some savings regularly.* This appears all but impossible to the family on a limited income. Yet it is a discipline that can be acquired, and it pays off in a nest egg for an emergency. Bank accounts, insurance, E bonds, and purchasing a home are all means to savings.

2. *Shop wisely.* Remember that price does not mean the same thing as value; indeed, the highest-priced goods may be of a poorer quality. Shop for durability rather than just for famous brand names. Study the findings of testing laboratories and research agencies before investing in purchases. Read the labels carefully. Shun the fancy, high-cost items in furnishings and appliances. Search out the simple, durable goods.

3. *Learn ways to save money at home* — and make it a habit. Many clothes can be sewed in the home. Gardening and canning will cut down on food costs. Pressing suits,

repairing fixtures, washing the car, and a host of other jobs can be done in the family without hiring services.

4. *Use your leisure time to increase your income.* Many folks have made their hobbies earn money in woodwork, sewing, printing, painting, and other lines. Some have found it possible to be part-time salesmen and to earn additional cash in that way.

This Matter of Christian Stewardship

In addition to the complicated task of teaching their children the value of money and somehow balancing the family budget, the Christian family have another large obligation. They must shoulder their responsibility by sharing with others who are in need; and in so doing they aid the personal and religious growth of their children.

One of the early chapters in childhood is the " my " stage. It is then that the ego becomes aware of itself; and a very healthy sign that is. But with gathering maturity the " my " stage should develop into a new and wholesome understanding of the needs of others. In the Christian home this growth takes place in a natural, unnoticed way.

For the Christian family have a stewardship. That means that they realize God is their Creator and that whatever they are and possess have come from him. It is therefore not by luck or self-made opportunity that they acquire their possessions. It is by God's gracious providence that they are able to use these gifts. So they dedicate gifts to God in Christ, who has given so much to them. According to their ability, they set aside a portion of themselves and their earnings for this cause.

The family that share an attitude in accord with this ideal are automatically handing on to the children something very precious. They will not be so preoccupied with the competition for attaining wealth. They will grow up with a sense of responsibility for others and their needs.

In recent years the churches have aided in this education through the Youth Budget Plan. In this plan children are trained in giving, are concerned with the mission of Christ's Church, and are given opportunities to name their own benevolences. They have "adopted" other children and young people by means of camp scholarships. They have become aware of needy schools and hospitals. They have sent food and raiment to the destitute.

Here again the value of an allowance is pointed up. The boys and girls learn to apportion a tenth or more out of their allowances to these highly worthy causes. They can take care of their own giving without a dole from Father.

How they respond in Christian stewardship is influenced, we again emphasize, by the pattern they have seen at home. It would be difficult indeed for parents to convey teachings of generosity if they have no such convictions themselves. They will hardly be successful in preventing their children from adopting a patronizing air in charity if they themselves have been giving condescendingly.

The sons and daughters in a Christian home will learn to share what they have because they care enough. This they come to do by habit, regularly, intelligently, wholeheartedly. They know something of the cause to which they give, whether it is a city mission or a Community Chest agency. Such compassion is not achieved overnight; it is slowly built up over the years at home.

They will have witnessed the Christian charity of their parents whose own giving is not simply added onto a bill-laden budget. It is provided for as a first principle in the family's planning. Proportionate amounts are set aside out of each pay check; and these are dedicated to Christian causes. This practice does reduce the amount available to spend on household needs, recreation, or clothing. Yet it also simplifies the financial problem in one way. The Christian family have a sense of values that makes items fall into place.

Because they first set aside that part of their earnings which is to go to the service of His Kingdom, the remainder of the budget benefits from sound planning. Priority has been given to the call of Christian service. When the family are agreed on this as a religious principle, their money problems may still be hard; but they gain new insights to handle them.

5: THE FAMILY
WORSHIP TOGETHER — HURRIEDLY

Family devotions need not be ugly or a bore, with people back to back each praying into a chair, with routine Scripture-reading done mechanically and worse expounded, with intercession offered in redundant platitudes; nor need it be long drawn out.
> — *Bernard Iddings Bell, in*
> The Parent, the Child, and God.

IN his frequently (all too frequently) quoted idyl, "The Cotter's Saturday Night," Robert Burns recalls the lovely, simple evening worship in a rural Scottish cottage. The farmer gathers about him his bairns and leads them as they praise God through chant, Scripture, and the lifting of prayer. He delivers a homily too:

> "'And, oh! be sure to fear the Lord alway,
> And mind your duty, duly, morn and night!
> Lest in temptation's path ye gang astray,
> Implore His counsel and assisting might:
> They never sought in vain that sought the
> Lord aright!'"

The beauty of this bucolic poetry may temporarily obscure from us the contrast between the conditions of that cottage and our own homes. But just try to pull together a contemporary American family of a Saturday night for a period of worship in the home! No simple rural economy exists any longer in this land of tractor, combine, and automobile. Our Saturday night social competition is very different from that earlier culture in which the Sabbath began with sundown on Saturday. Our jangling phones and jingling cash registers have complicated life to the extent that family worship seems artificial even among many churchmen.

Add to these uncongenial conditions the embarrassment of numerous parents, the irreligious background of others, and even the frank testimony of some that such a custom is to them an outmoded pattern that they dislike. Then we begin to see some of the complications (and there are yet more) faced by those who believe in Christian worship by family groups. Once homes displayed wall mottoes with the familiar words, " Christ is the head of this house, the unseen guest at every meal, the silent listener to every conversation." Most of them have long since been removed. George Hedley in his book *Christian Worship* suggests that when the interior decorators ruled such mottoes out of home *décor*, the thought behind those words also evidently went out of fashion.

Yet one who takes the trouble to investigate finds that many families grasp tightly some remnant of the once more general habit of worship in the home. It may be only grace at Sunday's dinner; but that much it is anyway. Or all that remains may be bedtime prayer regularly observed by the youngsters; yet that is something. What such families really need is instruction on how to pick up and go on from there.

The place for most people to start, it is commonly agreed, is at mealtime prayers. Schedules are hectic, and family members are spread from West Junior High

School to the East Division of the local mills during most of the day; but the family do occasionally arrive at the dining table at the same hour. Then it is that the family can briefly (yes, even if hurriedly) relate themselves to God through thankful prayer. The prayer may occasionally resemble Sir Jacob Ashley's famed petition before the battle of Newbury: " Lord, I shall be very busy this day. I may forget thee; but do not thou forget me." Yet the family group do have an opportunity to acknowledge God as the source of their life and of life's provisions. And that acknowledgment when followed through is the greatest thought given to man to consider.

In thanking God for our daily bread we are doing more than affirming our good fortune in economics. We are recognizing the presence of Christ in our midst. Prayer at mealtime is a profound symbol of our place in the family of God. The Bible recognizes bread to be more than food; it is in addition a means of God's grace. Bread also becomes an integral part of the sacrament of the Lord's Supper, and as it receives God's blessing, it speaks to us of Christ's life, and death, and resurrection. In this food we see the same kind of dependence upon the mercy of God as a baby feels toward his mother. Like the ancient Hebrew family, we too can pray: " Blessed art thou, O Lord our God, who bringest forth bread from the ground."

Grace at meals is expressed in many and various ways. Some families pray a memorized grace together. Others sing a hymn. In many homes, one person offers the prayer, each taking his turn. Some read theirs. Some offer a verse of Scripture or a prayer-poem. Some pray the well-loved Lord's Prayer that Jesus taught his disciples in reply to the request, " Lord, teach us to pray."

Those prayers are best which are worked out by the family as their own expression. Occasionally, though, they will wish to turn to traditional forms that are used in countless other homes. Some splendid, well-known graces are these:

> " Give us grateful hearts, our Father, for all thy
> mercies, and make us mindful of the needs of others;
> through Jesus Christ our Lord. Amen."

> " For what we are about to receive, dear Lord,
> Make us truly thankful.
> Grant us thy guidance
> Through the affairs of this day,
> And at its close — thy peace. Amen."

> " All eyes wait upon thee, O Lord,
> Thou givest them their meat in due season.
> Thou openest thy hands and satisfiest the desire of every
> living thing. Amen."

> " Bless us, O Lord, and these thy gifts, which we
> are about to receive from thy bounty, through
> Christ our Lord. Amen."

> " Lord Jesus, be our holy Guest,
> Our morning Joy, our evening Rest;
> And with our daily bread impart
> Thy love and peace to every heart. Amen."

> " Father in heaven, sustain our bodies with this
> food, our hearts with true friendship, and our
> souls with thy truth; for Christ's sake. Amen."

Worship in the home is sometimes advocated because it is " good for the children." Where that is the sole reason behind the practice of family worship, we can be fairly sure that it is *anything but* good for them. In a home where Christ is known and loved, however, worship can far exceed mere usefulness. It becomes a means of the grace of God.

Here at the hearthside a family together learn to pray to a God who is always near. To him they lift their thanksgiving and find that their home is transformed; for it is to be expected that in thanking God sincerely for the blessings of our home we find ourselves putting our home to his service.

Let worship in the home be informal, spontaneous if possible. It need not be solemn at all, but can be joyful — even fun. Little children should not be expected to sit still very long. The habit is strengthened by regularity, but it need not be limited to a special time or place.

Every so often one hears that family worship has died out. But the reports are exaggerated. Forms have altered, the schedule has changed; still the worshiping family continues. As long as there are Christian homes, there will be found within them the worship of God.

Four Errors Parents Can Avoid

Occasionally our own ideas of worship are not sufficiently mature; and our children have passed on to them false impressions we ourselves have too long harbored.

1. *For instance, we may assume that children at prayer are only mouthing words — verbalizing.* Dora Chaplin, in *Children and Religion,* reports the amusing outcome of such a misunderstanding when a little lad became fed up with what had become a meaningless routine. " You can all God-bless yourselves tonight," he grumbled; " for I'm tired."

Back of his complaint, though, is an indictment of those who had reduced his prayer experience to a series of pious blessings that held little reality for him. Children are capable of far deeper spirituality than most parents realize. The way their parents set the example in family worship makes a difference.

2. *The role of the parent in family worship is not just to "hear prayers."* There is something oddly sacrilegious about the father or mother who speaks of "listening to the child's prayer," as if there is no one else to hear them. It is actually part of the same error that is expressed in "saying prayers." For there is a wide distinction between saying prayers and praying.

If our children have their worship experience arrested at the point of merely *saying* or *hearing* prayers (however valid this may be as an early step), they dare not remain there lest we see our sons and daughters become religiously retarded children.

3. *We must not manipulate our family worship for ulterior reasons.* Irreverent as it is, some adults are not above the practice of using children's prayers for their own ends. Edmund Gosse tells in his autobiography, *Father and Son,* how as a boy he wished to go to a birthday party of which his father disapproved. "Lay the matter before the Lord," the elder Gosse admonished, evidently thinking this to be a subtle use of discipline. But when little Edmund emerged, he showed that he too had learned guile, and forthrightly piped: "The Lord says I may go"!

The mother who compels her resentful daughter to pray for pardon of a slight against Mother is also asking for trouble. We do not teach sincerity by creating spiritual pressures.

4. *It is easy to kill the worship habit by laughing at a child's awkwardness.* Of course, Sally will say something in a prayer which to adult ears sounds as funny as it would in conversation. It is not likely to promote a lifelong habit

of communion with God, however, if we show amusement.

Growth in worship, like all child development, is usually a step-by-step affair. It takes patience, understanding, and respect for the pace of the child.

In so many areas of child training, there is a noteworthy advantage to be found in beginning early. So too in learning to worship, it is easier for both the parent and the child if it is not too long postponed.

Some parents make it a habit to pause by the baby's crib and to voice a prayer of heartfelt thanksgiving for the wee one, asking a blessing upon this young life. Thus the baby, even as he begins to hear speech prior to learning to talk, knows something of reverence before he ever utters prayer.

When his understanding makes it possible, it is good to teach him simple words. A prayer for the nursery child is found in Sara G. Klein's *When They Are Three:*

> "Dear God, thank you today
> For food and rest and play. Amen."

As time goes on, the developing child may memorize a few such rhymed prayers, and then move on to the new stage of talking to God in his own words, and offering his part in family worship.

At this time the guidance of parents and church school teachers is needed. They can aid by talking over the meaning of worship with the child. The parent is helped by these talk-it-over sessions as much as (perhaps more than) the child; and they both grow spiritually as they read the Scriptures and express their prayers aloud.

The wise parent has a considerate technique when introducing new foods to a child. A small portion is placed on the plate at first. At the next meal where that dish is served, the portion is slightly increased. If the child rejects it, the objectionable item is removed and not offered again for some time. Many families find that this approach helps.

Now transfer of this same technique can apply to family worship. The worried parent who has trouble in getting Jackie to sit still during the Bible-reading, or encouraging Susie to pray, might well introduce worship gradually, offering brief satisfying experiences. It is not possible — or advisable — to expect of children a mature appreciation of family worship at once.

Some parents report that they find it helpful to paraphrase the readings in family worship so that even the toddlers can understand. The Scripture can be freely interpreted into the language that children use daily. The devotional readings are sometimes shortened or reworded for better comprehension by the entire family. This takes advance preparation. It is necessary first to read through the day's material and plan the necessary changes. Then the worship session is more meaningful to the whole family. Such a practice makes all the difference between the daily devotional's being a grown-up language or a familiar and welcome idea to the child.

Worship with Preschool Tots

Oddly, some of the finest opportunities for the education of a child come *before* enrollment in public school. It is in these fleeting preschool years, brief and demanding as they are, that some attitudes can become set for life. It follows, then, that if the child is led by observation in the home to see that lives can be inspired by faith, he himself will grow up with a readiness to accept the grace of God in Christ.

Family devotions now can be a beautiful experience, bringing the child to an appreciation of what worship truly is. The kindergarten age child is capable of expressing his own thoughts in short sentence prayers. And he has a real interest in the use of the Bible even to the extent of enjoying the music of some words he does not fully understand, such as the Twenty-third Psalm. He becomes familiar with a growing list of short verses from both the Old and New Testaments. These are related to his own experiences and often form the basis for discussion in family worship.

A prevailing mistaken notion has it that the Bible cannot be introduced to a child before he is three years old. Quite the contrary, the Bible is communicated to the young child long before he is even able to recognize it as a book. The Christian truth contained in the Bible is partly taught through family living in the Christian home; and the child begins to learn of love and kindness and integrity at an age when he is not yet talking. If the message of the Bible does not get into the child's experience at this early age, and if he does not see his parents make the Bible a constant resource in their own lives, when later he is able to read it for himself it may be difficult for him to correct those first impressions.

Soon the growing child develops an interest in stories. At this time a few simple Bible stories that are brief and can be told in short sentences should be read to him. The parent will find that these stories are called for, not just once, but many times. Stories of the Nativity, of Jesus blessing the children, of Jesus telling about God's love, are especially appropriate. In addition, a number of verses and portions of verses have a relevance to the small child if they fit into his own understanding.

The Bible stories ought not to be tiresomely told. This important introduction to the Book is to assure interest for both now and later years. If these first impressions are good ones, a young mind can grow with a realization that the Bible is life's most wonderful book and that its message is alive and essential for faith and practice.

Family Worship and the Grade School Child

The growing experience of grade school children makes them as quick to detect sham as to appreciate truth. This means that the family who want their children to love the Bible must themselves show that the Bible really means something to them. As George Bernard Shaw pointed out in *Misalliance,* a demanding and domineering mother who compels her child to learn the Sermon on the Mount could actually be teaching quite another lesson, namely, that the mother herself is not Christian!

The young child in a Christian home, on the other hand, begins to love the Bible when he helps to read it in family worship. He keeps finding new and deeper meanings to the simple verses he memorizes. He comes to know the Bible as the Word of God transmitted, not only in language, but also in life. He comes to know prayer as real communication with God because he witnesses it as just that when his parents pray.

By the time the child is in school, he becomes an explorer. Questions galore, investigations into new channels, and collecting odd items — all reveal an active and inquiring mind intent upon exploring the world around him. This stage, so bothersome to many parents, is tailor-made for family worship.

This natural bent for exploration can bring the Bible to an intimate place in the child's experience. The questions he is asking these days about life and its meaning are just the kind of questions that the Bible answers. And these can be discussed reverently in the family. That interest in collecting (at times so annoying to parents) can turn as easily to assembling and memorizing Scripture: the Ten Commandments, the Beatitudes, the First Psalm. Because his inquiring mind is ever active, he wants to be doing things. He'd rather look up interesting Bible stories himself than have them read to him. He'd rather possess his own copy than share his parents' Bible.

A. A. Milne's phrase suggests that the grade school child is "halfway up the stairs." Wherever he is he puts parents on their mettle. They need not dread his searching questions, which sometimes reveal their own lack of wisdom. Children and parents can learn together. They can read fascinating biography in the Bible, especially that chief biography of Jesus Christ. They can grow in their understanding of the Bible, and search for help to their difficult questions. They can get accustomed to using the Bible, and to worshiping day by day as they pray to God for his guidance, the guidance that is needed by parents and children alike.

Family Worship with Young People

Adolescence is a most trying time in a person's life, because it is then that one balances precariously between childhood and physiological maturity. As a result, the teen-ager is a being of vivid contrasts, *all* for or *all* against, sometimes wearing a mask of utter indifference. The adolescent is likely to be filled with doubts and questions about his faith and his place in the universe. This is normal, a healthy sign of growth. Capture his interest in a cause, and he will pursue it. Fail to win his backing, and no matter how lofty the project, he is capable of shrugging it off.

It is generally at this age that the young person unites with the church. This is a moment of high significance when decision is made about his commitment to God in Christ. It is at the same time a period of severe probing and deep concern. He now should mature in his ability to use the Bible and to understand its message. Prayer is coming to mean something much more important to him; and (this is no disaster) he is questioning the meaning of prayer. His increasing experience and keener insight enable him to find in Bible and prayer helps for his own living.

But what if this readiness to move into a wider realization of God's plan does not receive the encouragement it needs? What if parents fail their developing young people at this crucial hour, and hold them back from the faith for which they hunger? Then our young people grow up in an atmosphere already shallow in its Christian faith, promising little better for the future.

Christian character is nurtured, not in the fleeting moments of glorious experience, but in the common activity of everyday affairs, in a continuous, often undramatic, obligation. What counts in the long run is neither the few high points nor the blundering mistakes, but the general average of training over the years. Perhaps those daily times of worship have seemed prosaic to the family, yet in the long run they have been a powerful force for good.

When the young person is moving into his late teens, a maturing mind searches more deeply than ever for the mysterious why of being. Now come those times of disturbing questions whose answers seem so hard to locate. If the parents in this period can stand by ready to help, but allow their young people to seek the elusive solutions to their own problems, young people will grow religiously and morally as well. The family that pray together have a good chance to stay together in this trying period. The Bible records the quest of others who centuries ago sought out direction in these selfsame problems — and the Bible contains the chronicle of how, in God's grace, they found a way. Studying its passages can bring rich experience to everyone in the home.

The young person looks forward to a vocation, to marriage, to a life significant. If youths are shown the way, they can find in God's Word guidance for life, and a meaning in existence. Youth can be helped by home and church to see that God still loves, and seeks, and saves. The history of that process is best described in the Holy Bible.

Summary: Patience Does It

There is a remarkable readiness for reverence in our children. If a parent is alert enough to notice it in the questions that are asked, or the wistful remarks that are made, he will discover an awareness of God. At first the child's praying is notably self-centered, and this is to be expected. Only gradually does he develop a concern about others. But in time he learns to deepen his prayer thoughts. This comes with experience. It is abetted by imitation of adults whose spoken prayers recall the needs of the world's people, offer thanksgiving for the gifts life brings, or make petitions in accord with God's will.

When the child learns to read, he can begin to lead the family in worship by reading Scripture and prayers that appear in print. By the time he enters his teens, a firm foundation of Christian faith should be well begun. Far past the " give-me " stage of praying, now he is aware of the mystery of unanswered prayer. He realizes that not everything in life can be pleasant for him. He grows in his trust of a God who is ever close by, infinitely merciful.

Elton and Pauline Trueblood, in their book *The Recovery of Family Life,* contend that it is unnecessary to manufacture a religious program for the home because the family is inherently religious. What families really require is a reminder of their religious opportunity and some simple instructions to carry on.

Families who want to conduct Christian worship in the home would do well to review these pointers:

1. Keep the worship brief. Avoid long services by setting a time limit. Plan the period so that children and parents will all be present. It should be a time when there is the least anxiety about bus schedules or school bells.

2. Encourage the full participation of the children. They can read selections, offer ideas in discussion, ask questions. This will avoid boredom with worship.

3. Introduce new forms gradually, and if they meet with resistance, wait a while before trying them again. Avoid monotony by enriching the experience with varied usages: different versions of the Bible, sentence prayers, litanies, hymn singing, stories.

4. Intersperse Scripture-reading with ad libs that explain the verses or clarify the words.

5. Relate worship at home to worship at church because these two are closely connected. Teach small children at home to sing the hymns (e.g., Gloria Patri, Doxology, and frequently sung numbers), to know the Lord's Prayer and Church customs of worship. Then they will feel a part of the common worship.

6. Find a devotional guide suitable for your family. *Today, Thoughts of God for Boys and Girls, Prayer Time* are widely popular.

7. Persevere. At first, the practice of worship in the family group is difficult because it is new. Later it encounters difficulty with busy schedules. When obstacles are struck, parents will have to uphold for worship the same unflagging energy they apply to any other family standard, whether it be washing hands before dinner, or taking turns at the dishes. This way failure need not be expected.

6: PARENTAL PATIENCE AND ENERGY

I used to ask the busy mother of six young children, "Don't you get awfully tired and find that you need rest in the afternoon?" Because her work was the expression of her deep love, and because she had an inner rest so many of us know not of — "In Him I live and move and have my being" — she could answer, "Oh, I keep going and I get my second wind."
— *Josephine Moffett Benton, in* Martha and Mary.

MEREDITH WILLSON tells a fable about the band whose music so pleased a king that he opened to the musicians his royal treasury. With an expansive gesture he invited each of them to walk in and fill up his instrument with as much gold as he could hold. For the bass tuba player and the drummer that was lovely. But when everyone had got his fill, one man dejectedly departed, saying, "And there I stood with my piccolo!"

Far too many of us parents meet life's opportunities with a piccolo response. We accomplish much less with our families than we might because we lack time, strength, or inclination. We feel that our energies or our time will not permit us to make full use of the possibilities we confront. We excuse ourselves from living each day to the hilt by recounting the numerous complications that surround each hour. The result is a feeling of fatigue and futility. And these feelings in turn affect family life adversely.

To leave enough time and sufficient strength to accomplish our assignments, we must make careful choices between the things that are important and those which are not. The sad simple fact is that most of us waste our resources by making the wrong selections. We make a lampshade instead of helping Jackie to learn to ride a bike. We spend all day Saturday hoping to make an extra buck; but our children wanted to have a family trip.

Most of us live too near the surface of our abilities, dreading to call upon our deeper resources. It is as if a strong man were to do his work with only one finger. With all the fascinating gadgets and amusements of our day, we are easily tempted to " lay waste our powers " on unworthy objectives and activities. But life is too short, our children too valuable (and young so short a time), life's demands are too great to fritter our days away foolishly. As Robert D. Abrahams has suggested in his poem, " The Night They Burned Shanghai ":

> " Some men die by shrapnel,
>   And some go down in flames,
>   But most men perish inch by inch
>   In play at little games."

Instead of challenging us to triumphant living, the present crisis has been for some an excuse to adopt the slot-machine philosophy of life. They hope that by inserting a small coin they may someday hit the jackpot with a minimum of effort. Parents, who of all people should know better, have fallen into this same error.

In James Thurber's fairy tale *The Thirteen Clocks,* all the castle clocks had stopped one afternoon at ten minutes before five. Ever since that, time had been " then."

but never "now." Not only in that fictitious castle but in many a troubled life it never seems to be "now." Someday we will play more as a family, but not now. Some future time will suffice for those earnest conversations with the kids, not today. With no idea of how to balance their checkbook of time, too many parents squander their assets or even overdraw the account. It can happen in housework as well as in office work, at play as well as at labor.

For this there is no ordinary necessity. Each person each day receives a new portion of time — twenty-four hours. Every hour contains sixty minutes — for rich or poor alike, for adults as well as for the young. It is said that Andrew Carnegie was willing to offer two hundred million dollars for an extra ten years of time. No amount of wealth, however, can purchase this precious commodity. It is a gift. It cannot be hoarded. It must be used for good or for ill before the next deposit is entered. You can always count on receiving all the time there is, one day at a time. Even if you waste it, a new present of time will be handed you the following day.

Time is a marvelous value, steady, dependable, certain. To use its hours intelligently necessitates having a priority system as careful as the budget system for our money, described in Chapter 4. Decisions must be made in favor of those items which are of greater importance against those of lesser. But it pays off. In patience, in energy, in satisfaction, in accomplishment, in those important family relations — such a time budget is a boon.

We also need an energy budget. William James was one of the first observers to point out the curious phenomenon of "second wind" in our use of energy. His essay *The Energies of Men* insists that (1) most people give up their work activity too soon; (2) if only they would work on, there would come to them a new release of energy; and (3) if our project requires an unusual amount of energy, the supply is often increased without our knowing how.

The origin of this reserve fund is partly in the vast unused supply of our energy. Few of us live up to the limits of our ability. It is said, for instance, that the average person's usual mental activity takes up no more than twenty per cent of his brain capacity. The human brain is capable of continuous, hard activity without suffering any disability. It is now widely agreed that the so-called nervous breakdown does not result from hard mental labor, but from other factors such as worry, fear, and hatred. Likewise, as we are reminded in Josephine Benton's Pendle Hill Pamphlet, *Martha and Mary,* " work does not wear us out; but an emotional jag of feeling abused and overburdened very quickly produces a cumbered Martha."

Physical energy too is seldom used to the point of full efficiency, Professor James claimed, because we develop the habit of quitting when we " feel " tired. We ought to utilize the fuller amounts of energy within the bounds of good health and common sense. Our energy differs from our time in that the total supply available to people varies with the individual. Yet most people can probably push beyond their habitual level of work and be surprised as the " second wind " comes in to lift their production to new levels. How evident this is in the erstwhile fatigued mother of a sick child. She keeps going, no matter how tired she is, because she is buoyed up by the sheer necessity of her task. A father of only ordinary strength is credited in a news report with lifting the rear quarter of an automobile *because his son was trapped beneath it.*

Our love also lends power. When special demands are made upon us, special reserves are often discovered.

F. Scott Fitzgerald, in a low note of melancholy, once wrote, " There are only the pursued, the pursuing, the busy, and the tired." He was wrong. Without any sense of futile pursuit, feverishness, busyness, or tiredness, there are some who accomplish large tasks and move on to still others. This ought to characterize the Christian parent. Bred with the conviction that his possessions, his time, his talents — yes, his very life and its assignments — come as gifts from God, he feels a keen sense of obligation to use them correctly. Such a conviction consecrates life, work, and Christian family experience. It forces one to spend his energy and his days in those activities which would be judged worth-while by the will of God as we prayerfully understand it. Such a stewardship also keeps us awake to the personal values involved. And this prevents us from relegating the rights of our children to some time schedule. We can become uneasy, crotchety fathers and mothers if we count up each night what we failed to achieve instead of what deep satisfactions have come to our family this day.

In this we have a divine example drawn to our attention by Ralph Sockman's *The Fine Art of Using:*

" Jesus of Nazareth was master of the art of spending time. He never let it master him. He did not give the impression of dashing about Palestine trying to save time and keep to a schedule. He knew that his earthly working days were short. He said so. There was an air of urgency about him, but there was no feverish hurrying. He had time to sit and talk with individuals along the way. He paused to play with little children. He took time off to spend whole hours in prayer. But was it taking time off? Off from what? Ah, Jesus was not keeping to a calendar. He was fulfilling a life. And if we are to fulfill life, we must live our days to the full, so putting our whole selves into the present moment that the moment becomes a bit of eternal life. Thus the Master was above the passing of time. He measured the time he had to spend not by clocks and calendars but by the continuity and growth of life. Said he, ' My Father worketh hitherto, and I work.' He was going with God, and so he had all the time in the world."

Better than any other, the Christian ought to understand the nature of energy and of time. Convinced that these are gifts of God put into human hands for use, the Christian realizes the necessity for accounting for their proper expenditure.

The apostle Paul was a man of unbounded energy who made a tremendous record of service during his life. His was a singleness of purpose: " One thing I do, . . . I press on toward the goal for the prize of the upward call of God in Christ Jesus " (Phil. 3:13, 14, R.S.V.). A letter to his friends at Ephesus finds him advising them to be wise, " *making the most of the time* " (Eph. 5:16, R.S.V) .

Again, choices are demanded. Many things a Christian forgoes are not wrong in themselves. They are just not so worth-while as some others. The refusal of some, the acceptance of others, depends upon a standard of Christian stewardship. Time spent in quiet devotions, for instance, cannot be written off as time ill spent. Rather, it helps to set the pitch for the remainder of the day. From such an experience, be it devotional reading, thoughtful prayer, or silent listening to the Word of God, it is possible to return with new zest. True, the harassed mother or the rushed father may assume it better to allow devotions to slip until some distant Sunday; but when they arrive at this conclusion they forget that energies and abilities are by nature spiritual. A prophet centuries ago knew this truth and from a heart of sincerity wrote, " They that wait upon the Lord shall renew their strength; they shall mount up with wings as eagles; they shall run, and not be weary; and they shall walk, and not faint " (Isa. 40:31).

Challenge Calls Us Out

If we were to settle down to the level of living in which we are most comfortable, few of us would show any notable ambition. It takes a challenge to pull us above our customary rut. We are creatures of habit. We rarely desire to push our performance beyond the minimum. Yet some people find time enough and energy enough to get everything done that they ought to do. The busy always have time, we are often told. How do they do it?

They have learned to live on a higher level of power, and with the unusual stimulation of challenge they remain there. They find life worth living! Their work, their ideas, their love of family and home, their enthusiasms keep them in trim. And the more they do it, the better they are able to continue. They live in these greater heights of acomplishment because they are challenged by factors of enough importance to demand their full response.

Balzac worked sixteen hours a day, turning out seventy-four masterpieces of French literature in just twenty years. Douglas Freeman, according to *Time* magazine, arose at two thirty each morning in order to spend the early hours working on his biography of George Washington; then he drove to work, where he edited *The Richmond News Leader* the remainder of the day. Sir Winston Churchill, during the Second World War, worked an eighteen-hour day much of the time, administering a great land, preparing speeches, writing books, and even painting in oils.

The Christian, better than most, has the opportunity to

spend his life for some purpose that will outlive him. The parent in a Christian family has an even greater challenge. There has been placed into his hands by the grace of God a child whose growth and life will be his to influence. Why it is that an all-wise Creator with all the resources of the universe at his disposal should choose amateurs, mere parents, to do the most important of life's tasks, we do not know. We only know that it is God's plan; and that weary as we become, discouraged as we may get, this high calling is blessed by God Almighty. More than others, we ought to be able to feel the tug of challenge, unlocking our ability and energy to meet the task in the time given us. And we, above all else, should know how to reach for spiritual resources that are beyond our own. Underneath we can feel the Everlasting Arms.

SOME SPECIAL CONCERNS OF PARENTS

7: INTERPRETING SEX
TO OUR CHILDREN

Sex is, like any other tangible aspect of human life but more so than most because of its depth and breadth, sacramental in its function. Through the mystery of sex, God is revealed in the same process by which the depth of another, and consequently of oneself, is revealed in a new way. Sex is to the glory of God.

— *Seward Hiltner, in*
Sex Ethics and the Kinsey Reports.

JUST as children are curious about the trucks on the highway, the changes in the shape of the moon, or the pictures in magazines, so they are curious about sex. It is just as matter-of-fact as that; and their questions are just as natural as any of these others — unless parents by their attitude create an impression of shame or difficulty about it. This is "a delicate subject" only if the adult makes it so.

In this Kinsey era of frankness concerning the facts of sex, it would be unfortunate if our children hear discussions about life processes from others but not from their own parents. The task of explaining sex need not be so frightening to Father and Mother. And it does not have to be put in the imagery of birds and bees.

To begin with, parents can use correct names for parts of the body just as easily as they do for pieces of silverware. The child who has built up no self-consciousness about it will pick up one term as easily as another. For the tot to know the accepted names for reproductive organs does not necessarily mean he has to be given all the scientific details until he is ready for them. It does mean, however, that the first hurdle is crossed, because an understood and respectable vocabulary has been opened instead of baby talk.

Some parents are able to get through the age of heavy questions (about three through eight) with flying colors. They never bat an eye when the question might have been embarrassing. And, we may as well face it, such questions will be asked in public as well as at home. Just as a shrill little voice may sing out in the grocery store, " O Mommy, here's a kitty," so it can as easily shout, " Mommy, is the baby inside you now? "

One of the central sex questions is, " Where do babies come from? " The simplest solution is to answer the question, " Babies come from inside their mothers." The child has no hesitation in accepting the fact that the human egg, since it cannot be protected in a shell like the chick, is kept inside the mother's body until ready for birth. That's all there is to it for the little child. No explanations, no discussion. The chances are that he is quite satisfied and goes on to the next question, " Why do policemen have badges? "

It is unnecessary to reply with full details to the question of the younger child. If you did so, he might walk away during the lengthy explanation. What he wants is assurance more than knowledge. He is satisfied to know that there is a logical explanation, and that his mother or father will share it with him.

But suppose that still more questions come along about how the baby is born or how his life gets started. The technique of wise parents is to pursue the same policy of frankness and simplicity. " The baby is born through a special opening " is usually enough reply for the small child. An older child of grade school age could be told in the words that Hugh C. Warner offers for a mother in *Puzzled Parents:*

" When you were big enough, you came along through a passage which goes from that cozy, warm home inside my body to the outside world, just where my legs join my body. I was lying in bed when you were born, and as soon as Nurse had put on your baby clothes, I cuddled you and you had your first breakfast from my breasts, just here. You have forgotten that first meal, but I haven't. It's funny to think of it now when you are clever enough to use a spoon and fork for meals, isn't it? "

The father's role in parenthood may be more difficult to explain, though it may be already partly understood by the child from his own family relationships. In James L. Hymes, Jr.'s excellent Public Affairs Pamphlet *How to Tell Your Child About Sex,* he writes:

" Actions speak louder than words. Children who are deeply aware that fathers are important have a feeling basis for making sense out of the story of fertilization. They can realize in a jiffy why it takes two to make a baby. How? From having a daddy who has bathed and fed them, who has read to them, who has taken trips with them, who is more than a punisher-when-things-go-wrong. Such children can almost answer for themselves, out of their own good living, such questions as: ' Do you have to be married to have children? Can I have a baby by myself? ' They know for themselves that fathers count."

The curiosity of the young child may be annoying at times, but it is the signal of an inquiring mind. Be glad for it. Remember that if Junior doesn't ask his questions at home, he will seek his answers elsewhere. And it is much better to have those questions asked and answered in the home.

Generally when today's emancipated parents are asked questions about sex, they reply with readiness and with candor. But if they begin to withhold information, it is apt to concern the act of sexual intercourse. This should not be so difficult. Where there is an emotional block to relating this intimate part of the story, it is nearly always owing to the embarrassment of the parent, not of the child. Children are astonishingly matter-of-fact and uninhibited about any sort of new truth. And they can take this education better than we parents can give it. It should not be too difficult to explain that the way a baby gets started is by means of a fluid that leaves the father's body and enters the mother's where it meets the tiny egg. This is possible, the parent can continue, because a part of the father's body called the penis fits into a part of the mother's body known as the vagina, and thus the passageway is provided.

How much more should be added to the narration depends somewhat upon the age of the child, his readiness for learning, and of course his questions. That this act is an act of love between two people married to each other might be added. Careful explanation can handle the occasional request of the child to see his parents "start a baby." "No, you couldn't see us start a baby," the parent might reply. "It's a special time, when Mother and Daddy who are very much in love have this special experience. But that is the way you were started; and we're so glad you've come to be a part of our family."

This relating of the act of intercourse is the highest hurdle. The rest is commentary. The parent can explain, when asked why it is that only married persons may have babies: " It is to be fair to the little baby to make sure he has both a father and a mother in the home. It is in fact the will of God that only those who are married may perform this act."

Such full explanation, however, need not be volunteered by the parent. The preschool child's queries about sex ought to be answered frankly, and then dropped for the present. It is possible to tell too much. But if a particularly curious or somewhat older child persists in asking for the entire story, the parent should be ready.

Your own care of children may be the most powerful lesson that your child learns in sex education. As a matter of fact, you began the whole task long before you knew it. When you loved your little daughter and cared for her, you taught her family love. When you accepted as regular living the problems of bodily cleanliness of a young child, you taught that body functions are natural and common.

Mute circumstances themselves have been a boon to many families in helping with this teaching task. The advent of a new baby in the home is a natural for the explanation of the whole long procedure. Preparing for baby's arrival, caring for and feeding the little one when he arrives, create an education by experience that no words can excel. Older sisters and brothers really know about babies when they live through the home adjustments brought about by the new arrival.

Frequent assurances, such as, " This was the way Mother took care of you when you were a tiny baby too," may do much more than merely inform the older sister's intellect. It may also prevent jealousy from taking too strong a hold.

The Teen-ager

Answering the little child's questions about rudimentary sex facts and explaining some of the meanings behind these facts to teen-agers are two different problems. When the teen-ager has been honestly taught in his early years, he will not need that painful, confidential " man-to-man " talk we joke about.

Today's teen-ager is likely to be much more sophisticated about these matters. It is no longer of first importance (although it is always essential) for the parent to teach the *facts* about sex to teen-agers. But it is very important to give them moral and emotional background for this content. Here again the antiquated, puritanical attitude involving shame and embarrassment is apt to come to the fore. Theirs is the Kinsey era; and today's teen-agers are sophisticated in some knowledge, needy in other realms. Particularly do they need to be able to make value judgments as Christian young people. For some of them, questions of petting and freedom of sex activity present real issues. They are in need of a grounding in absolutes, "those grand old landmarks of morality." Knowing what sex is does not suffice for youth, nor even that sex is pleasurable (a detail most fathers leave out of their man-to-man talks). Young people need to be set straight on Christian sex ethics. They can be helped at church youth group discussions, in Hi-Y clubs, and by such books as Sylvanus Duvall's *Before You Marry,* or Roy E. Dickerson's *Into Manhood.* But they must be able to find help also from Christian parents.

Worry over youth morals is often wasted. Young people have a lot more sense than they are credited with, and their batting average is especially high when you consider that they are expected in today's world to work out a code of ethics in a more complicated setting than that of a generation ago.

For the parent who has got off on the wrong foot in his educational efforts with sex, there is no reason to despair. If the error has been in using untruths to explain life's processes, it is altogether possible to retract previous concepts with an admission of the previous misinformation. It can be explained that you are setting things straight with a now-you-are-old-enough-to-understand approach.

For those whose methods have been poor, there is a chance to turn it right. All the while it is essential to remember that the most potent lecture in successful sex education is the example of a fine and loving marriage between Father and Mother.

Don't's for Parents

Frances Bruce Strain, in *New Patterns in Sex Teaching,* has worked out a summary of rules from which the following are adapted:

"Don't turn boys over to fathers, or girls over to mothers. The parent who is questioned is the one who should answer.

"Don't separate children when answers are given, even if sex and age differ.

"Don't forbid young sisters and brothers to talk things over together.

"Don't consider a child punishable because he gives sex information to another child.

"Don't answer vaguely or in poetry. Young minds are direct and straight-thinking.

"Don't try to make answers complete from a biological standpoint.

"Don't wait to be asked a second time. Answer immediately

and to the best of your ability. Don't be afraid to say: ' I don't know. Let's look it up in the book.'

" Don't make an affair of it. Answer simply and naturally."

Parents Need to Understand Too

With all the current confusion about sex standards in the world today, one English educator has compared the situation to a football game played at night without lights. Both goal posts have been removed, and the confusion is confounded by the shrieking of whistles blown by a half dozen referees! It's a good metaphor at that. The effect of Dr. Kinsey's famed volumes on sex life has been to popularize a mechanical philosophy of life that considers humans as animals, and their acts as being without any moral significance one way or another.

The Christian philosophy of life, however, is anything but mechanical. The doctrine of election should save us from that. In the firm faith that God chooses us, that he knows us each by our first name, and has a more intimate knowledge of our ways than we have ourselves, the Christian views man in the image of God rather than as a mere striving creature.

One of the several difficulties with the mechanical concept of living is that it may lead the unthinking to adopt a standard of morality-by-averages. After enough data have been collected on some practice, it is easy enough to assume that whatever is frequent must be natural, and whatever is natural can be commended. This kind of false rationalization is familiar to us all. It goes in such terms as, " Everyone seems to be doing it these days, and you're just hopelessly odd if you don't go along with it." Such a formula is seemingly universal; it can be applied with equal effect to the playing of Scrabble or living in sin.

The validity of the Christian gospel, on the other hand,

is not concerned with the popularity of its requirements or even the frequency with which mankind shows its loyalty to God's law! Some of the gospel indeed seems quite offensive to modern man. Still absolute standards are not shaken by a law of averages, or a grand total of sums. The Christian should not be hoodwinked by some dishonest interpretation of the Kinsey reports into thinking that the prevalence of any particular sex practice means that he should join the crowd. Let it be clearly understood: the disciple of Christ has a higher loyalty than to morality-by-averages.

Parents of today's young people will have to re-examine their own position on Christian sex standards and make sure they know what they are talking about before they sit down to discuss the topic. It is good for us who are parents ourselves to recall Biblical teaching: that marriage is ordained by God to be between one man and one woman and that faithfulness to that condition is expressly enjoined; that the sex act, " one flesh " in Bible terms, is itself endowed with spiritual meaning and is created by God for the unity of the marriage relationship and for its fruitfulness; that God's blessing is present in Christian marriage, and that sex morals consistent with his will are expected not only in the marriage relationship but also prior to it.

Those who would reduce our sex ethics to the level of a mechanical philosophy of life see sex as only a physical matter wholly apart from God. The Christian, however, has a different conviction. He knows man to be created in the image of God, that he is redeemed through God in Christ, and that he finds real freedom and abundant life in God, who is his creator and his source. This is the good news of the gospel; and it is the framework of any Christian consideration of sex.

8: TO THE PARENT
WHO MUST WALK ALONE

Even when . . . divorce is necessary, if it is met honestly and courageously, the unfortunate effect is minimized. It has been widely and erroneously supposed that divorce is always ruinous to the children involved.
— *Katherine Whiteside Taylor, in*
Understanding and Guiding the Adolescent Child.

SOMETIMES a parent must walk alone. To her children, many a lonely woman has to act as both mother and father. In some cases, a father is compelled to shoulder the job of both parents. Whether the cause be death, divorce, hospitalization, or separation resulting from any of a dozen causes, such a parent carries a terribly heavy burden. The most common of these is divorce; for divorce has increased sharply in recent years, and it has struck all kinds of homes.

In contemporary America, upwards of 400,000 divorces and annulments are granted each year. Some sociologists fear that if this trend continues, approximately one out of every three marriages begun in the past ten years will ultimately be dissolved in divorce. Not only are the marriage partners involved, but also vast numbers of children. In fact, it has now been discovered that the number of children affected by divorce is rising even more rapidly than the divorce rate itself. This is the not unnatural result of the rising birth rate, as the number of marriages ending in divorce in a time of rising birth rate can be expected to involve more children.

The divorce system itself in the United States has brought down upon its head the combined wrath of Church and society. In current practice, it makes of this civil action almost a criminal offense because the court must find one party " guilty." The plaintiff and the defendant in a divorce suit are often prevented by their lawyers from speaking to each other or from showing any signs of reconciliation lest the divorce be impeded. This practice causes hard feelings, and harsher words. It forces couples to conform to certain prearranged charges so that the law will be satisfied. In order to work the case within the laws of the state, perjury is often encouraged. Sometimes the perjury is even caused by the court itself in the way grounds for divorce are cited. As a result, the charges are often trumped up, the testimony too frequently manufactured. Judges and lawyers know this; but they feel that there is little they can do about it under present conditions. As a kind of compromise with the system, most couples charge in a divorce suit the alleged condition of cruelty, or some variation of it. Cruelty in this case can mean almost anything in the wide gamut between assault and insult.

It has long been recognized that divorces themselves do not finish a marriage. They are often the legal result of already broken marriages. When a couple come to the divorce court they may arrive with a marriage that some time previously had been shattered. As long as so many marriages in this country are ending in divorce, there can be no optimistic view on the horizon that the American family is gaining stability. Quite the opposite seems to be the case.

Children of Divorce

Too often unconsidered, the children of divorce are perhaps its chief casualties. Somehow or other, many of the adults do pick up the pieces and go on. A majority of them, in fact, are remarried. But the children who have to suffer the effects of divorce without understanding the cause are among the most pitiful of the parties involved. They find themselves often shunted from one parent to another. They feel that they have no real home, no real love. Their own personalities can be stunted by the things that happen to them in the breakup of their family life.

One judge goes so far as to say that most of the juvenile delinquents who come before his court are the products of broken homes or of homes that are in the process of breaking. Children are deeply affected by the divorce of their parents. Many survive the ordeal successfully; and some even build strong marriages of their own as a result of their experience. But all of them bear somehow the marks of the experience. Neither the courts nor society as a whole have yet taken fully into account the effects to children in divorce. When they acknowledge that a divorce suit separates not only man from wife, but also parent from child, a beginning will be made.

A newly graduated social case worker found out very early in her career how children reacted to the separation of their parents. Broken homes, unstable family life were common in the underprivileged section of the city to which the young social worker had been assigned. Almost every unit in the teeming tenements housed a separated family. Many of the flats were entirely devoid of men.

Husbands had long ago deserted their wives and children. At other addresses there were some men, the second husbands of remarriage, stepfathers. Here, if in any place, one would expect community custom long ago to have conditioned the children to temporary family arrangements. Yet over and over again, when the social worker asked the children to name the wish they most wanted to come true, they replied, " To have my daddy home again."

Our children need the security of complete family living. For the young child the need to be wanted and to be loved by his two parents is as important to his welfare as milk, and rest, and sound teeth ever could be. On this security depend his health, his happiness, and his proper growth as a personality. That child suffers acutely who is withdrawn from his father and mother for any reason, be it evacuation in wartime, the death of a parent, or the deprivation of a parent by divorce and separation.

Home *is* different with just one parent. A family is not whole unless both the father and the mother are in it. There is more significance attached to this assertion than just the physical provision that each parent contributes to the home. The child is so formed, we noted in Chapter 1, that he greatly needs both of his parents for normal development. If he is deprived of one, the lack needs to be faced frankly and compensated for in some way.

Divorce in the U.S.A. more than any other one factor is responsible for the loss of this essential security. Since 1890, American divorces have increased in frequency *521 per cent*. The Federal Security Agency reports 3,500,000 paternal orphans under age eighteen in present-day America. Most of these children without fathers are the casualties of divorce. Between 175,000 and 306,000 children have been thrown into this vast number annually in the past decade. It is true that some of them do find happier relationships in new homes established by remarriage of their parents, but many of them do not. A proportion of this huge grouping of three and a half million are deprived temporarily of a parent who is in a sanitarium, or in prison, or in Army service. Yet they represent no more than five per cent of the whole. In one state (New Jersey), nearly one eighth of the total population is composed of children whose parents have been separated by divorce or desertion. Yet statistics can never reveal the real tragedy behind these family breakups.

Divorced men and women pay a high price. They are lonely, they feel defeated, they can become desperate. More needs to be said, however, about the price that the children pay in divorce and separation. They were not consulted about the marriage plans in the first place. They did not ask to be brought into the world; yet when the marriage is broken up they are among the chief casualties! Conflict, insecurity, and unhappiness can combine to plague their growing minds.

The child of separated parents can become the no man's land of grim civil war. Torn by loyalty to both parents, a youngster must always watch his conversation with each one, lest he somehow betray the other, awaken a burst of jealousy, or be grilled about his recent activities with the absent parent. The occasional visits permitted by the courts to the parent who is not granted custody of the child can be marked by unpleasantness and strain.

" Divided custody " is occasionally allowed by the court. Under such terms children spend part of the year with Father, part with Mother. For that little three per cent who have this arrangement it can be a brutal experience. The child may become a weapon used by both parents, who have grown to hate each other. What this does to children themselves is sad to behold. Hardened by such experiences, they become cynical, until as adolescents they are old for their years and grimly wise about the world.

Emotionally disturbed children are sometimes produced in broken homes — and it is no wonder. Their cases often come before psychiatrists. The destructive child who is the neighborhood's dreaded bully is from a home the father has deserted. Perhaps the listless, purposeless little girl was once the contested custody prize in a hot court battle between her estranged father and mother. It is probable that for some years preceding the actual breakup of the home, these children were part of the growing hostility, the tense relations between their parents.

The State of New Jersey, already referred to, in a recent year discovered that a full fifty per cent of the delinquents who had been arrested by police were the products of divorced homes. What proportion of the remainder came from estranged parents or intolerable home life is not known.

Boys and girls come to feel a sense of shame when their parents are not living together. They suffer the same real loss if one of their parents is dead, but their acceptance of death is somewhat easier. Death is a fact to be faced, not an emotional tangle that is hard to explain. Many a child makes up his own excuses for the condition of his home. Out of sheer imagination he will weave an explanation for teachers and friends that his father is dead, or that he is on an extended trip. It is a way of covering up what seems to him to be a fact too hard to face.

Add to this picture of emotional upheaval the usual

financial crisis that such children know as a daily gnawing experience, and you witness an underprivileged group indeed. Government aid to dependent children cares for more than 750,000 such boys and girls. Some receive support from their estranged fathers; but the median payments are just about $17.25 per week for a mother with minor children. To the child already scarred by the strife of a broken family, the uncertainty of physical welfare is another shock.

Desperately every child craves the family life he was meant to enjoy. It is expressed well by Frankie Addams in the play *The Member of the Wedding.* "All people belong to a 'we' except me," Frankie complains. "Not to belong to a 'we' makes you too lonesome." Seldom has the tragic loneliness of unhappy childhood been so well stated.

This one thing can be said with certainty about the child of a broken home — he is lonely. His loneliness may be evidenced in weeping, in so many words that clearly express the feeling, or in some behavior pattern that to the unpracticed eye appears simply as "naughtiness." Meanwhile the child himself may not even realize he is lonely, but may only be aware of a severe restlessness and bewilderment, a sense of insecurity.

It requires no psychiatrist to search out the cause for such loneliness. Its obvious source is the incompleteness of the family circle.

If the father is no longer in the home (and in most cases of broken families it is the father who is missing and the mother who rears the children), the family lacks an essential example of mature masculinity. This fatherly example, as we have seen, is essential because it sets a pattern for a boy to follow, or it enables a little daughter to develop her feminine arts on an appreciative male. If it is the mother who is absent from the home, the situation is even more critical. She supplies the warmth and affection so essential to the child's emotional development.

A Parent Faces It Alone

Loneliness is also the accepted fate of the parent who has been divorced. With the loss of a marriage partner, a companion in parenthood has also been lost. The result is that the spouse is intensely missed even if unfriendliness and quarreling had characterized the married life for some time previous. Now, somehow, a mother must play the role of both parents. In a few cases it is the father; but the economic standards of society usually place him in the workaday world and the woman in the home.

This task of adopting a new role, that of attempting to be two parents, is an impossible challenge. Some parents, however, do achieve a remarkable degree of success. Those who succeed best at it call to their aid the resources of family, neighborhood, church, and community. But, above all, they themselves must exercise the highest skills of parenthood and love.

Life's blows like life's blessings seldom come unmixed. Even the experience of separation, whether it is caused by death or divorce, or some other factor, such as a long hospitalization, is not without its compensations.

In an inspirational booklet of brief autobiographies, entitled *Yes, I Lost My Husband — But,* the women who composed its pages testify over and again to a strange strength they began slowly to acquire as they faced their hardest problems. It is as if the greater challenge has its own built-in resources.

One of these resources is a deeper love. As the mother

now lives for her children, she often transfers her conjugal love in some respects to her sons or daughters. Needless to say, there is a pitfall here, the possibility of indulgent affection and of spoiling the child. Yet the mature parent is able to center her attention upon the children's welfare, making up to them something of the loss suffered in a broken home.

So, too, the child's love is often concentrated upon the only parent he has left in the home, and the bonds between them can grow into firm ties of mutual support. Where the parent receives such love as a wholesome expression of affection, the chances for an overdependent clinging to mother's apron strings are considerably reduced.

Together Mother and children can and do face their world. In the process the children frequently seem to grow up faster than ever before. With maturer judgment a young lad begins to assume the manly jobs of the house: repairs, remunerative work, and helpful counsel. The young girl finds it necessary to do more of the womanly chores of the household, particularly if Mother works outside the home. Thus she too grows in the process.

The family is a marvelous institution. When trouble comes, the members can swiftly pull together and pool their resources to take care of an emergency. Many a distraught mother has turned to her parents or her brothers and sisters when her husband is gone from their home. The male companionship so craved by every boy can be provided by an Uncle George. The discipline problems insoluble by a lone parent can be talked out with experienced grandparents. The needs for additional money, arrangements for child care during working hours, plans for vacation trips for the children, and decisions about the myriad problems in the lives of growing youngsters can be discussed and solved with the help of the family. The broken home is an opportunity for rallying family solidarity.

Family life is undergoing vast changes in the twentieth century. Not the least of these is the higher rate of divorce and separation. However much the Church may deplore the trend and seek to prevent the breaking up of marriages, congregations do find among their number a greater proportion of divorced people. Even while the Church seeks through marital education and Christian family education to build homes that are stronger, it can aid the homes that are now broken.

The new-found vigor in the men's movements in our churches is sometimes turned toward projects of helping children from broken homes. A man can "adopt" a son in his church life. He can guide that lad in church activities, interest him in scouting, make sure that he gets to Sunday church school, and act as a big brother to the boy. Such a concept involves far more than the old pattern of escorting a son-for-the-evening to the annual father-and-son banquet.

The church owes it to the families within its parish to see that there are opportunities for club work and friendship groups under Christian leadership. The growing child actually needs a gang, and the deprived child craves friendship even more because he has lost a parent. The establishment of youth organizations may be an interdenominational or community-wide task, or it can be the project of one parish. But a good Christian education program does not overlook it.

The pastor himself is often the best counselor the church offers to broken homes. He has easy access to the family. He can talk with the children and help them in their adjustment. He can share the load with parents, aiding them with spiritual counsel, introducing to them the family welfare services, and assisting them in finding work. The pastor understands that the children who live in a calm and trusting setting, even if their home is broken, will find security.

Children do display a remarkable resiliency and toughness. They are capable of making difficult adjustments, and of coming through their experiences not permanently defeated. As a matter of fact, there are those instances in which youngsters have appeared to *gain* some notable value from even a broken home. Many a strong marriage has been buttressed by the resolution that this home will remain unbroken because one of the couple grew up as a child of divorce. Many adults are the stronger for having once been forced to mature rapidly in order to fill the gap left in a split family.

The process of growing up in such a home, however brutal the experience might be at times, is nevertheless an educational period of deeply etched lessons. How the child survives it all is largely governed by the quality of love that he finds around him.

One widowed mother writes of her current experience in rearing two children:

"As our family go on together meeting life in the future, we want the help of God and his Church; we also want such success in meeting our own problems that we shall have enough victory, courage, and energy to render efficient and joyful service."

Then, telling of prayer, this same mother goes on to say:

"One great source of inspiration in the past has been Prov. 3:5,6: 'Trust in the Lord with all thine heart; and lean not unto thine own understanding. In all thy ways acknowledge him, and he shall direct thy paths.' "

Somehow you don't worry about the children in that home. Problems they will encounter, of course. But with the firm faith which they witness daily in their home they can hardly be defeated.

9: IF YOUNG PEOPLE
DATE ROMAN CATHOLICS

It would be trite to say that the problems of mixed marriage are most readily avoided by avoiding mixed marriage. Yet this is true; and it may be well to impinge this platitude upon the thinking, unmarried, unengaged reader who is still free to make his choices without hurting anyone else or causing himself injury or pangs of conscience.
— *Henry A. Bowman, in* Marriage for Moderns.

PROBLEMS of family living do not diminish in number as the children grow older. They certainly change, as new challenges must be met. And the ability to meet the problems often improves as the years go hustling by. It is good that our problem-solving skills are sharpened; for the problems themselves often grow more complex as the family members grow older. With new responsibility and opportunity, there come new complications.

Susan's parents used to fret over her eating habits; now they worry about her dating habits. Sam's folks once despaired of his ever passing through the fighting stage in the fifth and sixth grades; now their greater concern is with his penchant for getting along too well with at least one of his companions — a Roman Catholic girl. It is obvious to anyone who has witnessed boy and girl friendship ripening into courtship, and courtship leading to marriage, that "entangling alliances" can begin quite early in life. Parents are rightly concerned when their teen-agers begin dating those of other faiths. The mixed marriage that so often follows mixed dating is fraught with difficulties; and the marital roadway is strewn with wreckage.

Clearly parents whose children are of dating age need to face realistically the issue of Roman Catholic-Protestant weddings.

Neither the Protestant nor Roman Catholic Churches have left any doubt that they regard interfaith unions with firm disapproval and as unwise in the extreme. As if the official Church positions so often enunciated were not enough, we have seen that the sociologists also have echoed counsel against marriage between parties of different faiths. They point to fact-finding surveys to buttress their stand that such marriages have the odds against them.

Definitive surveys were conducted in Michigan and Maryland by statistical sociologists, sampling more than 17,636 marriages. It was found that roughly two and a half times as many divorces grew out of Protestant-Catholic marriages as from either straight Protestant or straight Roman Catholic unions.

Not to be discouraged by the wreckage of Protestant-Catholic weddings, many young couples deeply in love glide blithely ahead in their matrimonial plans. They are determined to go into interfaith marriages anyway. And they do not lack a certain modicum of support.

In a widely read opinion poll conducted by *The Woman's Home Companion,* four out of five people replied that they believed "mature, intelligent people of basically different religious backgrounds can have a happy marriage." Even when asked if they would favor such marriage for their own children (this brought the question out of the hypothetical and drove it home), three out of five answered yes. Perhaps it is significant that in each of these queries, the Roman Catholics showed a greater readiness to accept mixed marriages than did the Protestants.

One Jesuit professor has analyzed the factors that tend to encourage Roman Catholics to marry Protestants. John L. Thomas, S.J., found that the American melting pot militates against isolated group cultures, and that in those areas in which Roman Catholics are greatly outnumbered, such weddings are frequent. So, too, as the immigrant Catholic families have improved their status with higher education and better income, they have more frequently entered into mixed marriage.

It is not unlikely that some Catholics favor interfaith marriage because the prenuptial agreement offers them considerable protection, arranging that nothing of their faith or their children's faith shall be altered. But sober fact, as we shall see later, has a way of influencing this arrangement; and Father Thomas has some grounds for his fear that " the Catholic population will be diluted."

Official statements inveighing against the mixed marriage are certainly not lacking. Among the numerous warnings two are typical. Both the Presbyterian Church, U.S.A., and the General Convention of the Protestant Episcopal Church agreed in a statement treating this subject. Their resolution admonishes " members of (either) Church against contracting marriages with Roman Catholics under the conditions imposed by modern Roman canon law, especially as these conditions involve a promise to have their children brought up in a religious system which they cannot themselves accept; and further, because the religious education and spiritual training of their children by word or example is a paramount duty of parents and should never be neglected nor left entirely to others, we assert that in no circumstances should a member of (either) Church give any understanding as a condition of marriage, that the children should be brought up in the practice of another communion."

Canons and encyclicals of the Roman Church also frequently remind the faithful of their obligation. Canon Law 1060, for instance, is a basic statement upon which a number of corollaries apparently have been defined: " The Church most solemnly and everywhere forbids marriage between a Catholic and a person enrolled in an heretical or schismatic sect. [This includes Protestants.] If there is danger of perversion for the Catholic party and the offspring, such marriage is forbidden by the divine law."

The experience of both church groups indicates that the mixed marriage can be a very unhappy marriage, and also that through it families often drift away from church. It is said that more than half of the men and at least a third of the women in such marriages drop their church connections altogether. But that is not all; the children born to these families can be pulled to and fro religiously until they become spiritual orphans — unclaimed by any church, and confused about their direction. Even in those Protestant-Catholic marriages validated by the hierarchy and regularized by all their required written pledges, the Roman Catholic Church estimates that they lose track of fully forty per cent of the children.

Occasionally the charge is leveled at the Roman Catholics that they encourage mixed marriage because it brings to them new converts. While it may be that some parish priest has hoped by this means to win new adherents, it can hardly be the view of the hierarchy. They have too much to lose, and the statistics show it. The very road blocks they throw in the way of a young couple contemplating interfaith matrimony are convincing enough that this type of union is to receive no encouragement.

Nevertheless, a large number of young people do cross the line of faith to marry. And the practice apparently is not only continuing, but is growing. The parent who finds his son or daughter contemplating such a step must speak carefully. By too vociferous a stand, he may force the very union he is seeking to block. Or if the young people do go ahead and marry, the family relations may be strained for many years to come. At the very least, however, it is advisable to urge a thorough study of what the Roman Catholic Church teaches about these unions. In many ways its outlook differs from our own.

Marriage, to the Roman Catholics, is a sacrament that can be validly celebrated only by their Church. A wedding in any other place (including Protestant churches) is not sanctioned, and leaves the couple theoretically living in fornication. If the Protestant refuses to become a convert to Romanism, the wedding is of a special nature. No nuptial Mass is said, not even a prayer is usually included in the service. The priest is not permitted to wear any vestments, to give any blessing. The service he reads is devised to show that this mixed marriage lacks the blessing of his Church. And the brief ceremony is almost never held inside the church, but in a rectory or home.

Much has been written about the statements that the priest requires the couple to sign before an interfaith marriage. Though brief, they are amazingly decisive. For all future time in this marriage, the Protestant girl marrying a Roman Catholic boy is expected to promise:

1. To rear all children from this marriage in the Roman Catholic religion, even if she outlives her husband.

2. To do nothing that would interfere with the religion of her husband.

3. To consider binding the ceremony as conducted by the priest, so that they present themselves to no minister for any additional service.

The Roman Catholic is expected also to sign a statement in which he pledges to attempt to win his Protestant helpmeet into his Church. The text of the antenuptial agreement, as it is called, is as follows.

ANTENUPTIAL CONTRACT AND PROMISES

To be signed in duplicate in the presence of the priest by the parties entering a mixed marriage, and by two witnesses.

To Be Signed by the Non-Catholic Party

I, the undersigned, not a member of the Catholic Church, wishing to contract marriage with the Catholic party whose signature is also hereinafter affixed to this mutual agreement, being of sound mind and perfectly free, and only after understanding fully the import of my action, do hereby enter into this mutual agreement, understanding that the execution of this agreement and the promises therein contained are made in contemplation of and in consideration for the consent, marriage, and consequent change of status of the hereinafter mentioned Catholic party, and I, therefore, hereby agree:

1. That I will not interfere in the least with the free exercise of the Catholic party's religion;

2. That I will adhere to the doctrine of the sacred indissolubility of the marriage bond, so that I cannot contract a second marriage while my consort is still alive, even though a civil divorce may have been obtained;

3. That all the children, both boys and girls, that may be born of this union shall be baptized and educated solely in the faith of the Roman Catholic Church, even in the event of

the death of my Catholic consort. In case of dispute, I furthermore hereby fully agree that the custody of all the children shall be given to such guardians as to assure the faithful execution of this covenant and promise;

4. That I will lead a married life in conformity with the Law of God and the teaching of the Catholic Church regarding birth control, realizing fully the attitude of the Catholic Church in this regard;

5. That no other marriage ceremony shall take place before or after this ceremony by the Catholic priest.

In testimony of which agreement, I do hereby solemnly swear that I will observe the above agreement and faithfully execute the promises therein contained, and do now affix my signature in approval thereof.

Signature of the non-Catholic party

To Be Signed by the Catholic Party

I, the undersigned, a member of the Catholic Church, wishing to contract marriage with the non-Catholic party whose signature is affixed above to this mutual agreement, being of sound mind and perfectly free, and only after understanding fully the import of my action, do hereby enter into this mutual agreement, understanding that the execution of this agreement and the promises therein contained are made in contemplation of and in consideration for the consent, marriage, and consequent change of my status, and I, therefore, hereby agree:

1. That I shall have all my children, both boys and girls, that may be born of this union, baptized and educated solely in the faith of the Roman Catholic Church. I understand that in case of my death, or in the event of a dispute, the custody of all the children shall be given to such guardians as to assure the faithful execution of this covenant and promise;

2. That I will practice my Catholic religion faithfully and will strive, especially by example, prayer, and the frequentation of the Sacraments, to bring about the conversion of my consort;

3. That I will lead a married life in conformity with the Law

of God and the teaching of the Catholic Church regarding birth control, realizing fully the attitude of the Catholic Church in this regard;

4. That no other marriage ceremony shall take place before or after this ceremony by the Catholic priest.

Signature of the Catholic party

The Church of Rome is unyielding in its demands on such a marriage. Interfaith weddings may proceed only after a special dispensation from the bishop. According to their Church law, these marital unions must be conducted under the same exacting standards as for any wholly Catholic family. So strict are these regulations, on paper at least, that the Roman Catholic partner can be permitted a separation from his spouse if the children are being educated as Protestants!

That the carrying out of these rules may be anything but strict is commonly known. The pope may decree that a woman's life is to be sacrificed whenever physicians must choose between fetus and mother, but actual experience is sometimes to the contrary. The priest may teach that the home's undisputed ruler is the man, but in actual practice it may be the familiar 50–50 companionate relationship. The priest may demand that mixed families rear their children to be Roman Catholic, but exceptions to this rule are legion.

As a matter of fact, many interfaith marriages are performed without the signing of the prenuptial agreement, the marriage service is read by a Protestant clergyman, and the children are brought up by Protestant teaching.

No small number of conversions from Catholicism come by means of marriage into the Protestant Churches. Where the Protestant stands firm on religious principle, it is often discovered that there is no necessity of signing away the faith of yet unborn children. This is a fact that parents should realize because it may make a real difference in the decision of those about to marry. Indeed, the Roman Catholic party is frequently seen to "come over." One young man, a Roman Catholic, put it this way: "When I saw what a Protestant upbringing had done for Nancy, I knew it would be good for our children too."

The Points of Strain

Marriage is a serious business, demanding maturity and grace in every case. But in a union between persons of differing religions, greater difficulty can be encountered. Some of the hard circumstances plaguing the interfaith family are these:

In-law troubles are immeasurably complicated if religious tension accompanies them. Grandparents have been known to arrange a secret Baptism for a baby when the parents are away.

A Protestant mother may sew a veil and confirmation dress for a sacrament she would not wish her daughter to have. And the child, in the inevitable clashes caused by home discipline, may resort to a religious defense in order to press a point.

The Roman Catholic in a predominantly Protestant family may see all the home life revolving about a culture he has never shared and fails fully to understand. He may hear his own children repeating some prejudice they have picked up, and be deeply wounded. The reverse can happen just as easily to the Protestant partner.

The couple who find they must go their separate ways religiously may find that they also begin to go their separate ways in other matters. Being unable to share some of the deepest things of faith, and prevented from speaking together with their children about religious matters, some inevitably drift apart. All marriages have their disagreements, and the vast majority survive them. But this disagreement is in the realm of faith. It is emotionally charged, and it takes wise people to handle it.

A Case History and a Prescription

Parents who see an interfaith marriage looming up in the family may have to go farther than learning about Catholicism. They may have to accept the situation of an interfaith marriage in their own household. If so, it will help them to know several things.

Jane is a young woman, reared a Presbyterian, who graduated from a Church-related college, and married a Roman Catholic with her eyes wide open. Fully aware of the many pitfalls in such marriages, she and Jack analyzed it all and prepared carefully for their home. Neither left the Church of his past, and both continue their religious activities as previously. They are happy in marriage and appear to have made of it a real success to date.

With candor Jane passes on this counsel to one who is going to marry a person of another religious faith in spite of all the evidence against the decision:

There are four main facts that must be ascertained *before* marriage:

1. Each person must learn the maximum amount about the teachings of the other's Church. This will enable each to understand better many things that come up later.

2. Each must discover the basic philosophy of the other toward his Church. There are strict Catholics and liberal ones, ardent Protestants and lax ones. This personal point of view may decide the degree to which a couple of two beliefs can share their faith.

3. Each should know everything he can about practices and customs of the Church of his betrothed. In daily life, the little things can be taken in stride, or can become upsetting — fish on Friday, special church services, financial appeals, choir rehearsals.

4. They must learn what the community attitude is toward each faith and toward mixed marriages in general. This may help a decision about where to settle. Neighbors and relatives could make life very unpleasant, if they had no sympathy with a certain religious point of view.

And there are two things that this knowing couple would prescribe for advance settlement:

First, before marriage it is essential to decide in what religious tradition the children will be reared, and (this is so wise for the parents watching their grown daughter step into a mixed marriage) *the prospective grandparents should be informed of this decision at the outset,* so that they can begin to accept it.

Second, the limits to which the couple may go in their missionary work on each other should be drawn. In this connection it is interesting to note that although the prenuptial agreement calls upon the Catholic to work for the conversion of his spouse, priests have been known to advise that this measure not be considered too literally, if it is likely to cause friction.

Jane and Jack plan on regular joint religious activities in which the entire family can unite. These include grace at meals, the Lord's Prayer with its slight variations, and occasional attendance at each other's worship.

They counsel that couples like themselves avoid at all costs the little criticisms and complaints to which we are all so prone. It is also wise, they insist, to pass up those frequent opportunities for humor and jokes about religion. That way lies danger. Here is an obvious place for the parents of such a couple to watch themselves, and to take care lest they foment friction.

Jane adds this word about her basic Protestant tenets. Above all, she stresses, it is necessary for her to maintain her own religious principles. To have an intelligent, virile faith is to be able to stand firmly when difficulties develop. There are enough problems attendant on any marriage (and more to encounter in the interfaith marriage) without also being shaky on one's religious foundations. And this is a place in which Protestant parents can be a strong support — but only if their own faith is firm and they are active in it. It will not help much for them to be adamant about protecting the interests of Protestant Christianity if they show no zeal for it in their own personal living.

Protestant parents who see their young people moving through courtship and love toward marriage with a Roman Catholic face an uneasy time. They know that they would wish to do nothing that alienates the son or daughter who plans such a marriage, but it is dreadfuly hard to avoid resentments. What can they do?

Parents do well to encourage a waiting period, during which the young people have a chance to make sure of their love and to learn more about the significant step they plan to take. Sometimes this amounts to a cooling-off period. One college girl agreed to an extension in order to study what was involved in marriage with a Roman Catholic. During this time of waiting she met another young man, a Protestant, and became sufficiently dubious of her intentions to break off her engagement. In time she married the Protestant boy.

Waiting until the engagement period to face these problems may prove to be a dangerously long delay. The time to avoid interfaith entanglements is in earlier years. Parents do well to discourage the companionship and dating with Catholics that can lead to matrimony. This, of course, is best done without nagging, but through careful assistance in arranging opportunities for young people to meet and date those of congenial religious background. (Often this involves sponsoring youth groups, chaperoning social events, and assisting in the Sunday church school.)

Moreover, it is sensible to make sure that through occasional conversation and by means of such pamphlets as *If I Marry a Roman Catholic* (which can be ordered from the National Council of Churches), the young people are informed early of the hardships encountered through marriage with Roman Catholics.

The paramount concern is this: that the Christian faith and life of the home is so wholehearted and so strong that positive influences are brought to bear from the very first. Then the issue of marriage into another type of faith may never come up. But if the problem does arise, this sort of firm religious rootage will be an asset, and the love that binds such a family will be capable of surmounting new tests.

Success in marriage isn't a result of freedom from problems anyway. A truly successful marriage is built by a couple who face their tests maturely and with Christian patience, working them out prayerfully together.

10: FACING THE WORLD
WITH A HANDICAPPED CHILD

Parents must learn that sooner or later they have to face
the situation, and the sooner they do, the better for all
concerned. They have to learn that bemoaning their fate
is not going to get them anywhere, nor is it going to help
their child in any way. They should do everything possible not only to adjust their child to the conditions under which he has to live but to adjust themselves.
— *Abraham Levinson, M.D., in*
The Mentally Retarded Child.

THE young mother loved children deeply. She always
had. When her own baby came, her joy was tremendous. The little one's beautiful eyes, her unusually pretty
features, her early signs of intelligence — all seemed to
forecast a happy, useful life during the years ahead. As
she grew through those early months of babyhood, she
was consistently healthy and always good. She was the
kind of child who drew murmured compliments from
complete strangers who were attracted to look into the
baby carriage.

When it was that the baby ceased to grow, the mother
could never tell. Ever so gradually she began to notice
occasional signs of difficulty. The child was slow in learning to walk; she was not yet talking at the age of three;
her span of attention was short. An incessant restlessness

seemed to possess her, pushing her on to activity that appeared purposeless. Her eyes, though lovely, were unresponsive. Her reflexes were slow and weak.

When the pediatrician called a consultation of doctors, the mother received their verdict with breaking heart. The little girl was retarded. She was feeble-minded!

Then began the long treks to other doctors, to specialists, to clinics, to hospitals. But nothing ever helped. At last Pearl Buck (for that was the mother's name) sorrowfully accepted the facts as they were, and set about adjusting to the crisis. The story of her disappointment and struggle is told in *The Child Who Never Grew,* published by John Day Co. in 1950.

Pearl Buck's pilgrimage from proud parenthood to despair, through scores of tests and consultations and interviews, is altogether too familiar to countless thousands of parents. For there are many others who have been through the same torture. Although they suffer in different degrees, the families who have handicapped children fully understand the heartbreaking problem. Their child may be feeble-minded; or he may be blind, perhaps crippled or deformed, deaf, spastic, or epileptic. The complications of handicaps seem endless. But among the families that have experience in them there is a common bond. It is the anguish of seeing a loved one thwarted.

In the parent of the handicapped child there is continual pain. He suffers from visions of what the life of this son or daughter might have been. Often he is worried over how the child would fare if both the parents were to be removed by death. Or he notices the concomitant difficulties that sometimes develop: emotional strain, inferiority complex, or pessimism.

These secondary characteristics are the ones that complicate family life. The long, unrelieved care of an invalid can put a strain on marriage, can lead even to divorce. It is possible for the healthy members of a family to become warped under the weight of their burden. Tempers grow short, smiles disappear as the home is geared to the needs of one member whose disability seems to crowd all other considerations aside.

But harmony in the home is important to the well-being of the disadvantaged child himself. Normal family life will benefit him and his brothers, sisters, and parents. The necessity of serenity and love in the home can hardly be overestimated. There are ways by which a family can make this all-important adjustment.

The Wrong Approach

1. *Ignoring the problem.* Whatever be the sorrow of the parent as he watches a deformed daughter try to make her way in life, there is no excuse for an attitude that would ignore the difficulty. It does not help to pretend that the handicap does not exist.

In *The Glass Menagerie,* by Tennessee Williams, Laura once speaks of her crippled condition. " Nonsense! Laura," her excited mother replies. " I've told you never, never to use that word. Why, you're not crippled, you just have a little defect — hardly noticeable, even! When people have some slight disadvantage like that, they cultivate other things to make up for it — develop charm — and vivacity — and *charm!* That's all you have to do! "

But refusal to face the truth has never been known to solve a problem. Quite the contrary, in this sense also, to know the truth is to be set free. Medical men are often astonished at the ability of people to " take it " when they learn the truth.

To know and to accept the reality of the situation are the first sure steps toward a remedy. But if families have indulged in lies, then the road to real recovery is doubly difficult. The discouragement is greater; the hurt seems deeper. To realize the nature of the problem opens the way to solving it.

Nothing is gained by retreating from the facts.

2. *Finding the blame.* Inevitable as it seems to be, it is just as fruitless for the parent to bemoan his fate and ask, " What did I ever do to deserve this? " To presume that the handicap of a child must be the punishment of a parent's sin is to present a gross caricature of God.

When this same false impression came up in regard to the blind man, according to John, ch. 9, Jesus criticized the question. " Master, who did sin, this man, or his parents, that he was born blind? " the disciples asked him. Jesus answered, " Neither hath this man sinned, nor his parents: but that the works of God should be made manifest in him." Once again had the need of man become the opportunity for God's grace.

There was a time when heredity was held to be the certain cause of any malformation in a child. Today this notion is considered by experts as an old wives' tale. Few abnormalities in children are now ascribed to heredity. A greater danger lies in this misunderstanding. A mother may begin to probe into her background, regretting that she took this medicine, or went to that doctor. A father may blame himself because of some past error, or perhaps even for marrying his wife at all. The upshot of this self-torture too often is that parents then take it out on the child himself, unwittingly punishing him for their self-recriminations.

Unexplained though they often are, these misfortunes

can occur in any family. Perhaps four fine healthy children are born into a home, and then an idiot. The difficulty may be traced to a hormone deficiency, to measles in a mother-to-be, or to a dozen other causes, or perhaps only to mystery. The important thing is not to fix blame but to take steps to help the child in the family.

3. *Expecting too much.* A third wrong approach to the child with a handicap is to push him to a performance beyond his ability. Because of family pride (rather than for the child's own welfare) he may be pressed to an effort of which he is incapable. Many an emotional disturbance in some disadvantaged youngster has been unnecessarily brought on by the overstrenuous insistence of parents. To demand that a cerebral palsy case feed himself neatly, or that a cleft palate should pronounce words exactly, is as unfair as it is senseless.

Cases are cited of feeble-minded children being taught to appear as if they can play bridge. Unenlightened parents have punished deaf children because they did not obey quickly. One father refused to walk with his son who had cerebral palsy, but only would follow behind him several paces because he was ashamed.

The gross mistakes of unfeeling parents can severely retard the child's adjustment and can add further psychological difficulties to his already hard road.

4. *Pampering the handicapped.* It is not kind, however, to spoil the handicapped child with too much service and pampering. He needs love, but he also needs discipline. The parent who turns his back on the daughter who has fallen may want dreadfully to help her up, but he knows that she must train her muscles to walk carefully and to get up herself. The mother who straps her son's deformed foot to the tricycle pedal is not cruel; she is helping him.

If the family wait on the child hand and foot, it is not unlikely that he will become a spoiled tyrant. Aside from the strain this puts on the family and on himself, it fails to equip him for the days ahead when he may have to stand on his own.

The Amazing Therapy of Love

To find the proper median between pampering the handicapped child and overworking his frail strength, one can turn to no fixed formula. Yet a general principle can be applied; it is old, tried, and proved. It is the way of love.

As much as any child, yes, more than most, the child with a handicap needs love. Not just the hugs-and-kisses variety of affection will do the trick. Love must show itself through patience and understanding. It is essential that such a child feel that he is wanted in a family, that he belongs there and is secure. On this basis must rest any treatment. The child requires love, no matter how repulsive may be his handicap, how trying his behavior.

The understanding parent will not threaten. A lame or deaf child already has enough fears. Nor will the child be expected always to show courage. The terrors of an affliction are great. If, at times, the youngster becomes frustrated and tearful, it should cause no surprise.

Authorities agree that the actual handicap is of less importance than the attitude that the family hold toward the child. Prominent among the requirements for such parents is that they think of their child first of all as a child, and only incidentally as a child with a handicap. It is important that these children be treated as persons, never as " cases " or as liabilities.

The child who is born with a withered arm is similar

to other children except in this one characteristic. With normal children he has much in common. Like them, he also needs a sense of security. He also requires love. He also seeks fun and pleasure along his own lines. The laws of learning apply to him as they do to others, but for him learning is more torturous. All in all, he is much more like other children than he is different from them.

The parents need not waste sympathy on these little ones. Sympathy for what they are missing (" Oh, it's such a pity that Jackie can't play ball! ") is misplaced and borders on the cruel. More constructive lines are available to the family than hand-wringing pity.

Incidentally, you can be assured that the parents' own attitude will be mirrored by others. The normal brothers and sisters of such a child will be as considerate as the parents teach them to be. But if one of the parents bears a secret resentment against this misfortune, no matter how carefully it is hidden, it will be noticed by the family. Probably, too, it will also be copied by other children in the family who will show much more openly their resentment and hate. Repeating the obvious is herein justified: the way to family love is by parental example.

There is more that parents can do than to guard their own attitudes. They can go to work on a constructive plan of action. It is not long before the parent who suffers with a child's handicap begins to discover others who are going through the same valley of difficulty. Together, in a fellowship of understanding, these parents can create mutual support. More and more now, parents' groups are being organized around such shared problems as cerebral palsy, poliomyelitis, or retarded mentality. In these circles they feel none of the embarrassment occasionally encountered when they are among parents of normal children. To report in such a group that "my boy spoke three new words this week" can mean more to those who understand the torture of a speech defect than a football letter means to an athlete's family. Parents' groups can study carefully the nature of a particular handicap and some of its remedies. They can become acquainted with handicrafts and the various methods of therapy.

Alone, each parent can go to work on the problems of nicknames and ridicule. If the cripple is dubbed "Limpy," or the obese "Fatso," it may hurt feelings. But the practice should draw no more sympathy than a scratch on the knee. Most of all, the parent should not interpret it as a personal insult.

It cannot be too strongly stated that the child's general health needs to be guarded, so that the handicap is not further complicated. It will be of real help to have good resistance to colds and a strong body to count on. On this point the authorities agree: when a good doctor is located in whom the parents have confidence, they should shop no farther but should keep close to him. The error is sometimes made of chasing from one medical man to another, dissipating money, and tiring the child. Somehow the family hopes to find one who will do what the others cannot. But when a competent specialist has begun treatment, his judgment should be respected.

The entire family feels better when it is doing something to relieve the strain of the illness or abnormality. Such action lessens emotional tension; it avoids a feeling of helplessness.

The parents are unwise if they drop all social and community activities in order to devote their full time to a handicapped son or daughter. It is for the very child's sake that the parents ought to keep up normal living, so that their outlook and disposition can be healthy enough to face the crisis at home. In so far as possible, the family ought to live as other families do, not ignoring the handicap, but adjusting it in the life of the child and the home. This is a far wiser measure than magnifying an illness to such proportions that it dominates all else.

Yet there are some compensations. " Our strength," Emerson claimed, " grows out of our weakness." Certainly there are innumerable examples of overcompensation in which the handicapped person worked so hard to meet his difficulty that in doing so he surpassed even normal persons. Ignace Paderewski had weak fingers. Glenn Cunningham had been maimed in the legs by fire. Charles Darwin actually said, " If I had not been so great an invalid, I should not have done nearly so much work as I have accomplished." It is alleged by many that handicaps have quite as good a chance to make a person as to break him. The number of handicapped people who have attained success make it appear that such a disadvantage is almost a qualification for success!

Some reasons can be traced for this seeming paradox. Those who are disabled are often able better to concentrate their energies. They have a more complete knowledge of their limitations and how to work within them. The maimed and the blind are accustomed to analyzing their movements. So skilled do some blind people become in stretching their other senses that their abilities are proverbial. Indeed, the Chinese have for years regarded the blind as almost supernatural persons because of their seeming miraculous abilities.

There is nothing to prevent a crippled boy from developing in music the skills he could not achieve in sports. The chronic invalid who has a rheumatic heart can nonetheless learn painting or excel in scholarship. One mother reports that of her four children the best adjusted is the least healthy — a girl who is lame from osteomyelitis.

Even the mentally retarded children offer compensations. Some of these are indirect. Pearl Buck learned from her daughter patience, tolerance, human compassion. Because their desires are less complex, retarded children are generally happy, and they can help to spread cheer to others. Not a few researchers in the area of childhood handicaps are those whose own children have suffered from some difficulty. This misfortune has spurred them to work in the field of their sympathy.

It is a truism to state it: were it not for our problems, we would have little progress. The insight is well put in the words of Lachlen McLachlen in the play *The Hasty Heart,* by John Patrick. Lachlen says, " I had tae be hurt tae learn." It is not necessary to suffer such hardships in order to show qualities of heroism and courage. But it is indeed possible to achieve a personal victory for the family within the adverse circumstances themselves.

That family which approaches this problem with a faith that God's grace is sufficient for it begins with the victory half won. Those who know the balm of prayer, and the strength from tapping spiritual sources far deeper than their own, report calmness and serenity in the midst of all their trouble.

REFERENCES

References

In this volume, reference is made to the following books, pamphlets, and magazines, which are listed in the order of their use.

CHAPTER 1

Paul Calvin Payne, *Beyond Courage,* Annual Report of the Board of Christian Education of the Presbyterian Church in the U.S.A., 1944.

Ogden Nash, "The Parent," in *Many Long Years Ago.* Little, Brown & Company, 1945. Quotation used by permission.

Lauretta Bender, "There's No Substitute for Family Life," *Child Study,* April, 1946.

Reuel Howe, *Man's Need and God's Action.* Seabury Press, Inc., 1953.

Plato, *The Republic,* in *The Dialogues of Plato,* Volume II, translated by Benjamin Jowett. Charles Scribner's Sons, 1907.

CHAPTER 2

Benjamin Spock, *Baby and Child Care.* Duell, Sloan & Pearce, Inc., 1946.

Ernest G. Osborne, *The Family Scrapbook.* Association Press, 1951. Quotation used by permission.

Graham Greene, *Confidential Agent.* The Sun Dial Press, 1945.

CHAPTER 3

Leslie Weatherhead, *Psychology and Life.* Abingdon Press, 1935.

Helen Parkhurst, *Exploring the Child's World.* Appleton-Century-Crofts, Inc., 1951.

Sidonie Matsner Gruenberg, *Your Child and You.* Fawcett Publications, Inc., 1950.

George Santayana, *Dominations and Powers.* Charles Scribner's Sons, 1951.

John Baillie, *Invitation to Pilgrimage.* Charles Scribner's Sons, 1942.

O. Spurgeon English and Constance Foster, *Fathers Are Parents, Too.* G. P. Putnam's Sons, 1952.

CHAPTER 4

Sidonie Matsner Gruenberg, *Our Children Today.* The Viking Press, Inc., 1952.

Henry C. Link, *The Way to Security.* Doubleday & Company, Inc., 1951.

Money Management: Children's Spending. Household Finance Corporation, 1952.

Elenore T. Pounds, "Teaching a Child the Value of Money" (Part I, "The Child of Preschool Age"), *Parents' Magazine,* January, 1952.

John Van Druten, *I Remember Mama.* Harcourt, Brace and Company, 1945.

Charles Dickens, *David Copperfield.* Dodd, Mead & Company, Inc., 1921.

J. K. Lasser and Sylvia F. Porter, *How to Live Within Your Income.* Simon & Schuster, Inc., 1948.

Arthur Miller, *Death of a Salesman.* The Viking Press, Inc., 1949. Quotation used by permission.

CHAPTER 5

Bernard Iddings Bell, *The Parent, the Child, and God.* Holy Cross Press, 1949.

Robert Burns, "The Cotter's Saturday Night," from *The Standard Book of British and American Verse,* edited by Christopher Morley. Garden City Publishing Co., Inc., 1932.

George Hedley, *Christian Worship.* The Macmillan Company, 1953.

Dora P. Chaplin, *Children and Religion.* Charles Scribner's Sons, 1949.

Edmund Gosse, *Father and Son*. Charles Scribner's Sons, 1908.

Sara G. Klein, *When They Are Three*. The Westminster Press, 1950.

George Bernard Shaw, *Misalliance, The Dark Lady of the Sonnets*, and *Fanny's First Play*. Brentano's, Inc., 1914.

Alan Alexander Milne, *Christopher Robin Verses*. Methuen & Co., Ltd., 1949.

Elton and Pauline Trueblood, *The Recovery of Family Life*. Harper & Brothers, 1953.

Today. The Westminster Press.

Thoughts of God for Boys and Girls. Connecticut Council of Churches and Religious Education, 1946.

Prayer Time, compiled by Edward D. Staples. The Upper Room, Nashville, Tenn., 1946.

CHAPTER 6

Josephine Moffett Benton, *Martha and Mary*. Pendle Hill Pamphlets, Wallingford, Pa., 1953.

Meredith Willson, *And There I Stood with My Piccolo*. Doubleday & Co., Inc., 1948.

James Thurber, *The Thirteen Clocks*. Simon & Schuster, Inc., 1950.

William James, *Memories and Studies*. Longmans, Green & Co., Inc., 1912.

F. Scott Fitzgerald, *The Great Gatsby*. Charles Scribner's Sons, 1951.

Ralph Sockman, *The Fine Art of Using*. Editorial Department, Board of Missions of The Methodist Church, 1946. Quotation used by permission.

CHAPTER 7

Seward Hiltner, *Sex Ethics and the Kinsey Reports*. Association Press, 1953.

Hugh C. Warner, *Puzzled Parents*. Student Christian Movement Press, Ltd., London (undated).

James L. Hymes, Jr., *How to Tell Your Child About Sex*. Public Affairs Pamphlet No. 149. Quotation used by permission.

Sylvanus M. Duvall, *Before You Marry*. Association Press, 1949.

Roy E. Dickerson, *Into Manhood*. Association Press, 1954.
Frances Bruce Strain, *New Patterns in Sex Teaching*. Appleton-Century-Crofts, Inc., 1951.

Chapter 8

Katherine Whiteside Taylor, *Understanding and Guiding the Adolescent Child*. Appleton-Century-Crofts, Inc., 1938.
Carson McCullers, *The Member of the Wedding*. New Directions, 1951. Quotation used by permission.
Carl Kardatzke, editor, *Yes, I Lost My Husband — But*. Board of Christian Education of the Church of God, Anderson, Ind., 1951.

Chapter 9

Henry A. Bowman, *Marriage for Moderns*. McGraw-Hill Book Co., Inc., 1942.
Morton Sontheimer, " Would You Approve Your Child's Marrying a Protestant? a Catholic? a Jew? " *The Woman's Home Companion*, March, 1953.
John L. Thomas, S.J., " Some Observations on Mixed Marriages in the United States," *Lumen Vitae*, 1951, Vol. 6, Nos. 1 and 2.
If I Marry a Roman Catholic. National Council of Churches, 1948.

Chapter 10

Abraham Levinson, M.D., *The Mentally Retarded Child*. John Day Company, 1952.
Pearl Buck, *The Child Who Never Grew*. John Day Company, 1950.
Tennessee Williams, *The Glass Menagerie*. Random House, Inc., 1945. Quotation used by permission.
Ralph Waldo Emerson, " Compensation," *Essays*, First Series. Houghton Mifflin Company, 1886.
John Patrick, *The Hasty Heart*. Random House, Inc., 1945. Quotation used by permission.